Averroes' Middle Commentaries on Aristotle's
Categories and *De Interpretatione*

Averroes' Middle Commentaries on Aristotle's *Categories* and *De Interpretatione*

Averroes [Ibn-Rushd]

Translated, with notes and introductions by
Charles E. Butterworth

St. Augustine's Press
South Bend, Indiana
1998

Cataloging in Publication Data

Averroës, 1126-1198.
[Talkhīṣ kitāb al-maqūlāt. English]
Averroës' middle commentaries on aristotle's Categories and De interpretatione / Averroës (Ibn-Rushd) ; translated by Charles E. Butterworth.
    p. cm.
Originally published: Averroës' middle commentaries on Aristotle's Categories and De interpretation. Princeton, N.J. : Princeton University Press, c1983.
Includes bibliographical references and index.
ISBN 1-890318-01-9 (cloth : alk. paper)
1. Aristotle. Categoriae. 2. Aristotle. De interpretatione. 3. Categories (Philosophy)—Early works to 1800. 4. Logic—Early works to 1800. I. Butterworth, Charles E. II. Title.
B749.A4E5 1998
160—dc21   97-37675
                                                                              CIP

∞The paper used in this publication meets the minimum requirements of the American National Standard for Information Sciences—Permanence of Paper for Printed Materials, ANSI Z39.48-1984.

FOR GABRIELLA

my own special archangel

CONTENTS

PREFACE

These are the first in a series of English translations of the Arabic text of Averroes' middle commentaries on Aristotle's logical works. Subsequent volumes will present English translations of Averroes' middle commentaries on Aristotle's *Prior Analytics, Posterior Analytics, Topics, On Sophistical Refutations, Rhetoric,* and *Poetics.* These, like the other translations in this series, are based on the new critical editions of Averroes' Arabic text which are being prepared and published in Cairo under the auspices of the American Research Center in Egypt. As with these other translations, the goal here has been to present the English reader with an understandable and coherent version of Averroes' text, a version that remains faithful to the thought of the original Arabic while retaining the character of standard English expression.

Averroes' commentaries on Aristotle can make a claim to the attention of learned people on at least two counts. The first derives from their own intrinsic merit as philosophic treatises and will be explored at greater length in the introductions to each of the translations. The other has to do with their significance as works representative of a distinct tradition of Aristotelian scholarship and is related to the curious manner in which Aristotle's writings eventually made their way to Western European centers of learning. Though not without some relevance to this whole issue, there is no reason to recount at length here the fascinating and controversial tale of how a set of Aristotle's writings was passed on from Theophrastus to Neleus, preserved intact by the latter's heirs for an extraordinarily long period of time, then transmitted to Apellikon, seized by Sylla when he took Athens, sent to Rome to be entrusted to Tyrannion, and finally made available to Andronikus of Rhodes who newly catalogued and edited them.

Far more germane is the fact that Andronikus' edition had so little subsequent influence in Western Europe. Indeed, historians of the tradition of scholarship agree that Greek versions of Aristotle's texts disappeared shortly after the middle of the sixth century. Apart from copies of Marius Victorinus' Latin translation of the *Categories* as well as copies of Boethius' Latin translations of the same work, plus the *De Interpretatione* and part of the *Prior Analytics*, Aristotle's works were simply not known in Western Europe until about the middle of the twelfth century. Yet Boethius, who died in 525,[1] must have had access to the Greek text of all of Aristotle's works as well as to those of Plato, for he proclaimed his intention of translating all the works of each and then of proving that they were in basic agreement on all important issues. Though Isidore of Sevilla, Julian of Toledo, Archbishop St. Ouen of Rouen, Hadrian, and Theodore of Tarsus all bear witness to knowledge of Greek and of Greek authors in their writings, they are exceptions. So, too, are Alcuin and Joannes Scotus or Erigena, the former for his familiarity with Homer and the latter for his familiarity with Plato's *Timaeus* as well as for his Latin translation of Dyonysius the Areopagite. Among the numerous factors contributing to this lack of interest in Greek and Greek learning in general and in Aristotle and Plato in particular, three are pre-eminent: the closing of the school at Athens in 529 by order of Justinian, the fall of the Roman Empire along with the break between Rome and Constantinople, and the single-minded emphasis on the Scriptures and the Church fathers within the Roman Catholic Church to the exclusion of philosophic and pagan authors.

Aristotle's writings found a much more receptive audience on the other side of the Mediterranean. The efforts of Ptolemy Soter to entice members of the Peripatetic school from Athens to Alexandria shortly after Aristotle's death, coupled with those of his son Philadelphus to build the

---

[1] Unless otherwise specified, all dates are C.E.

library and the famous Mousaion, made Alexendria a great center of learning. The school which arose there and survived until the second decade of the eighth century was especially interested in the study of Aristotle's writings. Commentaries by Theophrastus were preserved and complemented by those of Alexander of Aphrodisias, Porphyry, and Olympiodorus. Nor was the one at Alexandria the only philosophic school in the East. Learning flourished in Constantinople, Edessa, and Antioch. In fact, when the Alexandria school was forced to close, it moved to Antioch. By the latter part of the sixth century, many of Aristotle's writings had been translated into Syriac. This activity continued and eventually led to the Syriac translations being rendered into Arabic. By the time the school moved to Baghdad in about the tenth century, successive generations of translators had revised the earlier versions or made entirely new ones, so that a very rich legacy of Greek philosophy and science was at the disposition of the nascent philosophic movement within the Islamic world. This legacy, substantially enriched and improved upon by commentaries as well as by other parallel investigations, then moved across North Africa and up into Spain with the spread of Islam.

From Spain the legacy returned to Western Europe by means of translations from Arabic into Hebrew and then into Latin beginning in about the middle of the twelfth century. Writings of Aristotle previously unknown in Western Europe were followed by writings of al-Kindī, al-Fārābī, Ibn Sīnā or Avicenna, and then in the beginning of the thirteenth century by those of Ibn Rushd or Averroes. Even after the Latin conquest of Constantinople in 1204 and the discovery of new Greek manuscripts, the most complete translations of Aristotle's works were still those done from Arabic. Without exaggeration, the beginnings of scholasticism in the later Middle Ages can be traced to the effect this newly found legacy had upon Western Europe, especially to the effect it had upon such important thinkers as John of Salisbury, Saint Thomas Aquinas, Albertus Magnus, and Roger Bacon.

Consequently, English translations of these works directly from the Arabic, as with the translations presented here, provide access to a very important tradition in the history of philosophy. Moreover, insofar as it is now evident that the Arabic and Syriac translations were based on Andronikus' Greek edition of Aristotle's writings, as are all of the Greek copies of Aristotle's writings which have been recovered and used in the numerous editions of his writings since the first third of the nineteenth century, the translations as well as the commentaries based on them bear witness to an essential element of continuity within these otherwise separate lines of transmission. However, the fact that there were two distinct Aristotelian traditions for so many hundreds of years must not be forgotten. Comparisons between the commentaries of Boethius and those of Averroes, for those works on which commentaries by both exist, will shed light on the precise differences between these two traditions. So, too, will direct examination of Averroes' commentaries, for he had access to the writings of many commentators unknown to Boethius and commented on far more writings of Aristotle than Boethius. Finally, to the extent that the writings of Averroes and other Arab philosophers prompted the scholastic movement of the later Middle Ages, which in turn led to the modernist attack upon Aristotle in particular and the ancients in general, an understanding of those antecedents to modernity is essential for its correct appreciation.

Although the text of Averroes' *Middle Commentary on Aristotle's Categories* has previously been translated into English, it seems appropriate to offer this new translation because it is based on a new and more comprehensible edition of the Arabic text as well as because it offers a more faithful and more readable English version of that text. The merits of the new Arabic edition can be explained by giving a brief account of it. Those of the new translation will hopefully become evident when it is read.

Father Maurice Bouyges published his edition of Averroes' *Middle Commentary on Aristotle's Categories* in Beirut in

1932. At that time, only three manuscripts of the Arabic text were known to exist: Florence, Biblioteca Medicea Laurenziana, CLXXX, 54; University of Leiden Library 2073; and Cairo, National Library, Manṭiq 9. Using the Leiden manuscript as a base, Father Bouyges established his edition according to the readings of these three manuscripts. When Professor Mahmoud Kassem began his own edition of the text, the discovery of one other manuscript had been announced: the Teheran Mishkat 375. Though Professor Kassem did not live long enough to see his project to fruition, his goals were achieved in his name by the preparation of the edition upon which the translation presented here is based. Shortly after work began on the edition of the *Middle Commentary on Aristotle's Categories* in 1974, following Professor Kassem's death a year earlier, the existence of three times as many additional Arabic manuscripts came to light. Because some of these manuscripts had been erroneously identified and thus incorrectly catalogued and others had only recently even been catalogued, they were not known to either Father Bouyges or Professor Kassem.

One manuscript, no. 2237 in the Oriental Public Library at Bankipore, was identified in the catalogue as an abridgement by "Fārābī of the Arabic translation of Aristotle's work on logic by Ibn Isḥāq." However, a close look at the incipits and excipits of the manuscript as presented in the catalogue revealed that it was actually a copy of Averroes' middle commentaries on Aristotle's *Categories, De Interpretatione, Prior Analytics,* and *Posterior Analytics.* A similar examination of the different passages given of manuscript no. 462, x, in the *Catalogue Raisonné* of the Buhar Library led to the discovery that it, too, was a copy of Averroes' middle commentaries on those four works of Aristotle rather than "an incomplete work of logic" containing "an abridgement of Aristotle's *Kitāb al-Maqūlāt,*" as it was described in the catalogue. Both of these manuscripts, like the Cairo manuscript known to Father Bouyges and Professor Kassem, are written in clear Oriental script and date from the eighteenth century. And the same attention to the substance of the incipits and excipits suggested that yet another manuscript, the Dublin

Chester Beatty 3769 (listed as "AL-QIYAS, the *Analytica Priora* of ARISTOTLE, translated by THEODORUS") contains the same middle commentaries by Averroes as the Bankipore and Buhar manuscripts. It, too, is written in a clear Oriental script, but may date from as early as the sixteenth century.

The other newly discovered manuscripts are located in Iran, eight in Teheran and one in Mashhad. Although properly classified, their existence has come to light only now as the result of the publication of new catalogues and of hand-lists of library holdings.

It is clear that all of these manuscripts and the Cairo, National Library, Manṭiq 9 are related. All are written in Oriental script, either *nastaʿlīq* or *naskh*, and are quite recent. All contain only Averroes' middle commentaries on the first four books of Aristotle's *Organon*: the *Categories, De Interpretatione, Prior Analytics,* and *Posterior Analytics.* Moreover, from what a close comparison of the Cairo, Teheran Mishkat, Teheran Shūrāy Millī, Bankipore, and Chester Beatty manuscripts suggests, these manuscripts differ from one another very little. Generally speaking, they are carelessly copied and replete with scribal errors. Only on rare occasions do they offer better readings than the older Florence and Leiden manuscripts, which date at least from the fourteenth and sixteenth century respectively. Yet they seem to be ultimately based on manuscripts which have the Leiden manuscript as their source. In the *Middle Commentary on Aristotle's Categories*, for example, the Cairo, Teheran Mishkat, Teheran Shūrāy Millī, Bankipore, and Chester Beatty manuscripts have readings that agree with those of the Leiden manuscript more than half again as frequently as with those of the Florence manuscript.

In addition to the greater knowledge of the text afforded by these additional manuscripts, however infrequently they contain major variants not found in the previously known manuscripts, the following considerations called for the text to be edited anew. First of all, praiseworthy as it is, the Bouyges edition is not free from errors. Secondly, because of Father Bouyges' curious reluctance to introduce anything more than the simplest elements of punctuation and his apparent diffidence about signalling the different steps in Averroes' argument by means of paragraphs, it is an extraordinarily difficult text to follow. What is more, despite remarkable attention to minute details, Father Bouyges never bothered to help the reader locate Averroes' own textual cross-references. Finally, it seemed that a simplified critical apparatus, a set of notes that would clearly identify the source of a given reading and the basic variants, would be far more helpful to the student of Averroes than the extremely elaborate, but often confusing, critical apparatus adopted by Father Bouyges. There really is no reason, after all, to signal all the misspelled words in each manuscript or the numerous instances in which a particular scribe neglected to provide the dots for a given letter. And there is even less reason to record each and every correction introduced by the scribe or whoever else re-reads the manuscript.

In sum, the new edition differs from that of Father Bouyges in that it strives above all to alert the reader to the form and substance of Averroes' argument and to provide the ready tools for making a judgment about significant variants in the manuscripts. The latter goal has hopefully been achieved by the use of a simpler and more accessible critical apparatus. Steps toward the former goal include the identification of passages to which Averroes alludes in the course of his discussion and the division of his text into numbered paragraphs in order to make the steps of his argument clearer. To avoid insinuating too much editorial interpretation into the text, a simple rule was followed with respect to the paragraphing: a new paragraph was indicated only where the subject clearly changes or where Averroes breaks the flow of the discussion by speaking in his own name (e.g. *naqūl*) or by citing a passage from Aristotle (e.g. *qāl*).

An even greater difference between the new edition and that of Father Bouyges arises from the fact that the former is based primarily on the Florence rather than on the Leiden manuscript. Three reasons seem to warrant this change.

First, the Florence manuscript appears to be the older

of the two. Although both are very well preserved and written in a clear *Maghribī* script, neither is dated. Yet whereas the ownership of the Leiden manuscript can be traced to the latter part of the sixteenth century, a note on the first page of the Florence manuscript identifies as its owners individuals known to have lived in North Africa during the eighth century, A.H., that is, the fourteenth century, C.E.

Secondly, internal dating within the manuscripts suggests that the manuscript from which the Florence manuscript was copied is something like a revised edition of the manuscript which gave rise to the Leiden manuscript. At the end of the *Middle Commentary on Aristotle's Rhetoric*, it is stated in the Florence manuscript that the commentary was finished in the month of Muḥarram, A.H. 571, that is, in the month of July, 1175 C.E. The corresponding passage in the Leiden manuscript speaks of the commentary having been completed in the month of Shaʿbān, A.H. 570, that is, in the month of February, 1175 C.E., or about six months earlier than the date mentioned in the Florence manuscript. In a number of instances this understanding that the two manuscripts stand in relation to each other as text and revision helps to explain their different readings. The student of the text can almost picture Averroes struggling to make his argument and his reasoning tighter. And this line of thought also explains why the Florence manuscript offers, generally speaking, better stylistic variants than the Leiden.

However, the major reason for preferring the Florence to the Leiden manuscript as the basis for the new edition is the conviction that it offers better substantive variants. That of course is a judgment which will have to be tested by the reader. Still, it might be of interest to consider the following. Of the 264 notes in the text, not counting those relative to the different divisions of the work, 84 concern substantive textual problems. In these 84 cases, the readings of the Florence manuscript are preferred 54 times or about two thirds of the time, whereas Bouyges prefers them only 30 times or a little more than one third of the time. As nearly as can be determined, his predilection for the readings of the Leiden manuscript in those 24 contested instances skew the sense of Averroes' argument.

To the extent that these considerations clarify the need for a new edition of the Arabic text of Averroes' *Middle Commentary on Aristotle's Categories*, they also argue persuasively for a new English translation. Averroes has, after all, presented a very faithful explanation of Aristotle's text in this commentary. Because he adheres so scrupulously to the basic structure of the text and endeavors to comprehend why Aristotle ordered his discussion in this particular manner, the reader must be made aware of these features of Averroes' commentary. At the same time, Averroes permits himself occasional reflections about Aristotle's purpose and surmises concerning the philosophical character of such an introduction to logic. These, too, must be brought to the reader's attention. Whatever else might be said about it, the present translation clearly offers the most faithful English version of Averroes' original Arabic text.

Although Averroes' *Middle Commentary on Aristotle's De Interpretatione* has never before been translated into English or into any language other than Hebrew and Latin, it has previously been edited. Shortly before the publication of the edition on which the translation presented here is based, Professor Salīm Salīm's edition appeared. However, the numerous false readings of the basic manuscripts and frequent selection of the wrong variant occurring in that edition revealed the need for another edition. In addition, Professor Salīm's punctuation of the Arabic text frequently makes it difficult to discern Averroes' teaching.

On the other hand, the edition of the Arabic text standing behind this translation is characterized by the same attention to detail and concern for setting forth Averroes' own teaching as the Arabic edition of his *Middle Commentary on Aristotle's Categories* which has just been described. The manuscripts used in that edition were also used in this one. As with that edition, primary attention was focused on the Florence Bibliotèca Medicea Laurenziana CLXXX, 54 and the

University of Leiden Library 2073 manuscripts, the Florence manuscript being taken as the foundation.

In the translation of this work, every effort has been
taken to render faithfully the form and the substance of
Averroes' argument. Such a concern is especially important
here because, generally speaking, Averroes has taken remarkable liberties with Aristotle's text. He rarely mentions
Aristotle by name and quotes him directly only five times.
At that, two of those five "quotations" have no parallel in
Aristotle's text. Even in the course of explaining a point
made by Aristotle, he frequently breaks away in order to
explore different questions at greater length than Aristotle
apparently deemed necessary. Finally, the basic problem
of the conventional nature of language, as well as the whole
issue of the way different kinds of sentences imply or contradict one another, are explained far more thoroughly by
Averroes than by Aristotle.

Here, too, then, the reader must be able to distinguish
clearly between what Averroes says in his own name and
what he says in Aristotle's name. Hopefully, the concern
with language and attention to formal or structural details
which characterize this translation will permit the reader
to make such distinctions.

In keeping with this goal of presenting an understandable
and coherent yet faithful rendering of Averroes' Arabic
into English, every effort has been made to translate basic
terms in the same way. To make it easier for the English
reader to recognize the Aristotelian character of many of
these terms, those used by J. L. Ackrill in his translation
of Aristotle's *Categories* and *De Interpretatione* have been
adopted where appropriate. When it has not been possible
to maintain the same terminology without doing violence
to English, the reader has been alerted to the difficulty by
means of a brief footnote.

Footnotes have also been used to identify textual allusions made by Averroes in the course of his argument. The
texts themselves have been divided into numbered paragraphs in order to reflect the different stages of the ar-

gument, and the tables of contents (The Order of the Argument) give a summary account of each paragraph. These paragraph divisions were first used in the editions of the Arabic texts on which these translations are based, but are not indicated in the manuscripts of Averroes' commentaries that have reached us. The manuscripts only provide an indication of formal breaks in the argument corresponding to parts, sections, and chapters in the case of his *Middle Commentary on Aristotle's Categories* and into chapters and discussions in the case of his *Middle Commentary on Aristotle's De Interpretatione*. Even though the former commentary is unique insofar as Averroes has carefully divided Aristotle's text into parts and each part into chapters or into sections and chapters, it was frequently still necessary to introduce the further subdivisions into paragraphs.

Just as the convention of paragraphs as known to us was not used in medieval Arabic texts, neither was formal punctuation used to divide thoughts into sentences or clauses. Instead, linguistic formulae were used to denote the steps of an argument corresponding to clauses and sentences, and yet other linguistic devices signalled the change in thought which corresponds to our use of paragraphs. While the paragraphing introduced in the Arabic edition has been followed faithfully, liberties have been taken with the punctuation. Because Arabic sentences tend to be long and quite complex, it sometimes made more stylistic sense to break them into smaller units for the English reader. At all times care was taken so that nothing but style was affected. The religious formulae found at the beginning of the treatises in the Arabic manuscripts have not been reproduced here: they add nothing to the arguments, nor is there any greater reason to believe that they come from Averroes than from the scribes. Finally, when appropriate, the relationship between Averroes' commentary and Aristotle's text has been indicated by placing in the left-hand margin at the beginning of the paragraph the corresponding passage in Aristotle (using the page and line references of Bekker's 1831 Berlin edition).

In sum, every possible step has been taken to present

here, in English, texts which are faithful in letter and in spirit to Averroes' original Arabic works. The old doubt of *traduttore, traditore* cannot, however, quite be laid to rest. To be sure, there are many instances where Averroes' language could have been recast so as to be more consonant with usual English usage. But that could not be done while at the same time adhering to the principle of consistent translation for key terms. Since the goal in texts of this sort is less eloquence than accuracy of thought, a certain heaviness does prevail—a heaviness which is, I hasten to add, equally present in the Arabic text. In the end, perhaps, there is only one thought which can console the translator of such writings, namely, how much better he understands the text now that he has labored to put it into his own tongue. At this point, then, all he can do is trust that this understanding is accurate and that it is faithfully conveyed by the translation, securing this understanding and passing it on to others being after all the primary purpose of such scholarly activity.

It is a great pleasure to express my gratitude for the assistance and sound council that Professor Muhsin Mahdi has offered throughout the many stages of this project, especially for his thoughtful reading of an earlier version of these translations and his numerous helpful suggestions. I would also like to state how much I appreciate Professor Michael Marmura's many valuable suggestions for revising these translations and for frequently helping me to understand the text better. Finally, I am very happy to express my warm thanks for the material support provided by the National Endowment for the Humanities, the primary sponsor of this project, and for the intelligent manner in which it has administered the grant which permitted this work to come to fruition.

AVERROES'
MIDDLE COMMENTARY
ON ARISTOTLE'S
CATEGORIES

INTRODUCTION

I

If the number of times a question is asked is any indication of its significance, anyone introducing others to a commentary such as this must begin by stating whether it contains anything that differs markedly from the original exposition. Clearly, the very tone of the question suggests that there is no reason to bother with a commentary if it offers nothing new. Yet for the sake of serious learning and perhaps even for the sake of true philosophical inquiry, both the question and the inference need to be resisted. Novelty, after all, has only recently come to be admitted as a criterion for judging contributions to human knowledge. The merit of apprehending the insights reached by a predecessor distinguished for his wisdom and passing them on in more accessible terms can be reasonably slighted only to the extent that truth is deemed to be changing. And however much this position is now generally accepted within the community of learners, it is far from being self-evident or adequately defended.

Still, simply because the question of whether there is anything new in Averroes'[1] commentaries on Aristotle does enjoy such favor today, an answer cannot be refused. The unequivocal reply, especially if one compares Averroes' commentaries with those of Abū Naṣr al-Fārābī (870-950) and Abū ʿAlī Ibn Sīnā (980-1037), is that he is not very innovative with respect to the way he handles Aristotle's text.[2] On the other hand, to the extent that he distances

[1] Abū al-Walīd Ibn Rushd, known in the West as Averroes, was born in 1126 and died in 1198.

[2] For a discussion of the novel manner in which al-Fārābī and Ibn Sīnā treat Aristotle's *Categories*, see my "Averroes's *Middle Commentary on Aristotle's Categories* and its Importance," *Miscellanea Mediaevalia, Sprache und Erkenntnis im Mittelalter*, XIII (1981), pp. 368-370 and 370-371.

himself from his immediate predecessors by writing commentaries distinguished by their fidelity to Aristotle's thought, Averroes is highly original. When the circumstances prompting Averroes' decision to undertake commentaries on Aristotle's works are recalled, his tactic comes into sharper focus. As the story goes, Abū Yaʿqūb Yūsuf, the Almohad ruler in North Africa and the Andalusian provinces from 1162 until 1184, persuaded that earlier Arab authors' explanations of Aristotle were inadequate and that the existing Arabic translations of his works were too confused, sought out Averroes and asked him to explain the texts of Aristotle in a coherent fashion. Although the tale is usually evoked in order to indicate the high esteem in which Averroes was held by his sovereign, it also suggests that Averroes' basic motivation in setting about to comment on Aristotle's works was to explain those works and thereby to meet a critical intellectual need rather than to display his own creative thinking.

Something like this is apparent also from the opening lines of most of those commentaries, for Averroes frequently begins his works by stating that the purpose of his investigation is to explain what Aristotle said about a particular subject. Thus, in the prologue to his *Long Commentary on Aristotle's Physics* as in that to his *Long Commentary on Aristotle's Posterior Analytics*, Averroes explains that he has undertaken such a commentary because no complete commentary from any of his predecessors has come down to him. And he indicates quite plainly that he intends to set forth Aristotle's teaching, nothing more or less.[3] Similarly,

---

[3] For the prologue to Averroes' *Long Commentary on Aristotle's Physics*, which no longer seems to be extant in Arabic, see Steven Harvey, "Averroes on the Principles of Nature: The Middle Commentary on Aristotle's Physics I-II" (Ph.D. dissertation, Harvard University, 1977), p. 457. Though long believed to be lost in Arabic, the text of Averroes' *Long Commentary on Aristotle's Posterior Analytics*—or at least a large portion of the first part of that commentary—has now been discovered. Heretofore miscatalogued, the manuscript's true character was recognized by Helmut Gätje and Gregor Schoeler when they looked more closely at the text itself; see "Averroes' Schriften zur Logik. Der arabische Text der *Zweiten Analytiken* im *Grossen Kommentar* des Averroes," *Zeitschrift der deutschen Morgenlän-*

in his *Short Commentary on Aristotle's Physics* as well as in those on the *De Anima* and on the *Metaphysics*, Averroes explains that his goal is to give a condensed version of the most salient features of Aristotle's teaching in each of those works.[4] And in this commentary, Averroes' first statement is a declaration that he intends to comment on Aristotle's ideas; it is followed by his explanation of what he considers to be the basic order of this book.[5]

II

It seems, however, that there is something problematic about these ideas, for Averroes attenuates his statement of purpose by warning that he will study them to the best of his ability. The explicit references to one particularly valuable insight of al-Fārābī and to an erroneous interpretation he made as well as the attempts to resolve problems which apparently stymied earlier commentators—for some reason Averroes says nothing throughout the commentary about Ibn Sīnā or his writings—suggest just how problematic Averroes and others found this treatise. Nonetheless, he does not think it important to supplement Aristotle's work

---

dischen Gesellschaft, 130 (1980), pp. 557-585. The opening lines of the manuscript are quite similar to those of Averroes' *Long Commentary on Aristotle's Physics*: "The purpose of this discussion is to comment on the *Posterior Analytics* which is known as the *Book of Demonstration*, for no long commentary of it from any of those who interpreted it has come down to us." (N.B., the word translated as "to comment" is *sharḥ*, i.e., the word for "long commentary" or, since it functions as a verb here, "making a long commentary.")

[4] See *Kitāb al-Samāʿ al-Ṭabīʿīy*, in *Rasāʾil Ibn Rushd* (Hyderabad: Dāʾirat al-Maʿārif al-ʿUthmānīyah, 1948), p. 2. For an English translation of the *Short Commentary on Aristotle's Physics*, see Harvey, "Averroes on the Principles of Nature," pp. 401-438. See also Averroes *Talkhīṣ Kitāb al-Nafs*, ed. Fuʾād al-Ahwānīy (Cairo: Maktabat al-Nahḍah al-Miṣrīyah, 1950), p. 3; and Averroes *Talkhīṣ Mā Baʿd al-Ṭabīʿah*, ed. ʿUthmān Amīn (Cairo: Muṣṭafā al-Bābīy al-Ḥalabīy, 1958), p. 1. As is now generally recognized, the editors of the last two volumes erred in labeling each a *talkhīṣ*, or middle commentary; the proper title would be *jawāmiʿ* or *mukhtaṣar*, i.e., short commentary.

[5] See below, *Middle Commentary on Aristotle's Categories*, para. 1.

in any manner: though he did write a middle commentary on Porphyry's *Eisagoge* at a later date, he makes no reference to the *Eisagoge* here; Aristotle's *Categories* is unquestionably the work with which to begin the study of Aristotle's logic.

Averroes first divides the *Categories* into three parts: an introductory section in which the ideas that function as principles and definitions are presented, a main body of the text in which the various categories are investigated at some length, and a final part in which rules and attributes relevant for all or most of the categories are discussed. The introductory part discusses the arguments presented in the first four chapters of Aristotle's text as it is now known to us; the second part investigates the arguments of chapters 5-9; and the third part delves into Aristotle's explanations in the last six chapters of the *Categories*. Averroes is exceedingly meticulous about the way he divides his investigation in each of these parts. Thus the discussion of Part One is divided into chapters, that of Part Two into sections and chapters, and that of Part Three into sections—which are also denoted as discussions—and into chapters as well. Many of these chapters are quite short and, with the exception of those in Part One, do not correspond to the chapters into which Aristotle's text is now divided. Whereas the five chapters of Part One in Averroes' own text roughly correspond to Aristotle's chapters 1-4, the forty or forty-two chapters of Averroes' Part Two and the fifteen chapters and discussions of his Part Three far exceed the corresponding divisions within Aristotle's text. Perhaps to compensate for this overwhelmingly structured discussion of the *Categories*, Averroes confines his comments on the fourteen chapters of Aristotle's *De Interpretatione* to five chapters of his own, of which only the first is further divided into discussions. However that may be, it should be noted that in Part Two and Part Three of his commentary on the *Categories*, Averroes' sections—that is, the entities which are further divided into chapters—correspond almost perfectly to the actual chapters of Aristotle's text as it is now known to us.

It is worth paying attention to these external features of both texts because we are really in no better a position with respect to Aristotle's text than was Averroes. Though we do have access to a Greek text that is almost identical to the Arabic translation of the Greek which Averroes may have used, he demonstrates that he also had access to commentaries composed by adherents of the school in Alexandria which are now lost to us. The divisions within the text of Aristotle as it has come down to us have no authority, nor does anyone know their origin. One of the manuscripts containing the Arabic translation of the *Categories* which Averroes may have used, the Paris Bibliothèque Nationale Or. 2346, is free of any such divisions. The divisions brought to the text by Averroes must come, then, either from his reading of those lost commentaries or from his own understanding of how Aristotle's text should be divided. Whatever the source, the importance he attaches to those divisions is clearly manifested by his insistence on explaining in summary fashion the parts of the book, the chapters of Part One, the sections and then also the chapters of the sections of Part Two, and the chapters of the first section or discussion of Part Three.[6]

In two of the three instances in which Averroes' organization of Aristotle's text is at variance with that text as it has come down to us, Averroes' interpretation seems sounder. Thus when he divides Aristotle's Chapter Three into two chapters, one in which the problem of predication is discussed and the other devoted to the explanation of subordinate and co-ordinate genera, he formally separates what deserves to be distinct.[7] Even when he does the opposite, that is, when he brings together into one chapter what had been relegated to two chapters, he seems to capture the underlying thread of Aristotle's reasoning. When discussing opposites, Averroes embraces as part of the same chapter the discussion of contraries which is now presented as a separate chapter. And he is correct to do so, for con-

[6] See below, paras. 1, 2, 17, 18, 34, 49, 65, and 88.
[7] See below, paras. 2, 12, and 13, with Aristotle *Categories* 1ᵇ10-15 and 16-24.

traries are one of the four kinds of opposites enumerated at the very beginning of the discussion and referred to at various reprises in the explanation which follows. To accord the final discussion of them the status of a chapter breaks the continuity of the preceding explanation and makes it difficult to discern the basic theme of this part of the treatise.[8] Even in the case where Averroes may be faulted, it is only because he does not go far enough in his restructuring of the text. At the end of the detailed investigation of the categories of substance, quantity, relation, and quality, Aristotle says a few words about the category of doing and being affected, even fewer about the category of position, and then concludes the discussion by explaining that what he said at the beginning of the book about the rest of the categories—when, where, and to have—was sufficient. This whole discussion constitutes the ninth chapter of Aristotle's text. Though Averroes concurs with Aristotle's explanation, he relegates the discussion of doing and being affected to a separate section, as he had done with the categories of substance, quantity, relation, and quality. He does the same with the category of position and then concludes that section with a few remarks about the categories which have not been discussed.[9] Yet the same concern for balance which led him to accord distinct ranks to the discussion of each of the other categories should have prompted him to introduce yet another section for this final group, however small that section might be.

A final external feature of Averroes' commentary which warrants consideration is his use here of the utterance *qāl* (he said), meaning "Aristotle said." According to current scholarly opinion, the particular characteristic of Averroes' middle as distinct from his short and long commentaries is the ubiquitous presence of this utterance. It is certainly

---

[8] See below, paras. 88-103, esp. paras. 89, 90, 91, 96, and 99, with Aristotle *Categories* 11ᵇ16-14ᵃ25, esp. 11ᵇ19-22, 11ᵇ35-12ᵃ25, 12ᵇ26-13ᵃ17, 13ᵇ12-19.

[9] See below, paras. 84-85, 86, and 87, with Aristotle *Categories* 11ᵇ1-8, 8-10, and 10-15.

present in this commentary. Yet of the 105 paragraphs in which one might reasonably expect to find the expression, it occurs only in 42. (The eight paragraphs excluded from this comparison are those in which Averroes summarizes the chapters or sections to follow. Even with those paragraphs excluded, the utterance occurs here in only about 40 per cent of the instances in which it should reasonably be found according to the received opinion about Averroes' style.) Were someone to object that such a finding only shows how inaccurately the editor of the Arabic text has transmitted the basic thrust of Averroes' argument, a sufficient reply would derive from following the same procedure for the chapters and sections into which Averroes himself divides the text. Of these, there are fifty-six chapters and six sections or discussions: five chapters in Part One; forty chapters in Part Two, plus two separate sections which function as chapters; and eleven chapters in Part Three, plus four other sections or discussions which seem to have the status of chapters. Now of these 62 instances where one might reasonably expect to find the utterance *qāl* if current scholarly opinion is correct, it occurs only in 28, that is, with a frequency of something like 45 per cent.

Apart from casting into doubt the notion that Averroes' style is marked by this use of a formal stylistic device, such comparisons suggest the merit of pondering what Averroes wants to achieve by his use of the utterance *qāl*. In order to determine the function it serves within this and other commentaries, what needs to be done, apparently, is to compare the instances where he uses that device with those where he does not, as well as to investigate whether he is paraphrasing Aristotle when he uses the device but is not doing so when he does not use it. However, my intention here is to do nothing more than raise that question. Given the place of this essay as an introduction to a translation of Averroes' *Middle Commentary on Aristotle's Categories*, it seems more important to turn to a discussion of what one actually learns from the text about both Aristotle's and Averroes' thoughts on the subject at hand.

III

Averroes deems it as important to note that Aristotle's mode of argument in the *Categories* is non-technical or even popular as to explain that it is the first of Aristotle's books on the art of logic. His reference to the latter characteristic seems to help explain why he chooses to begin his own study of logic with this work rather than with something like Porphyry's *Eisagoge*, but it is not so immediately evident why he considers the other characteristic to be so significant. Yet he points to it twice in his opening remarks, stating in both instances that Aristotle's discussion of the categories is couched in terms of what is "generally accepted." And he returns to that same theme a number of times later in the commentary. Each time, Averroes indicates that Aristotle has resorted to arguments based on "unexamined and generally accepted opinion" or to merely "persuasive" (as opposed to technically sound) arguments because they facilitate instruction.[10] Yet nothing in Aristotle's text suggests that his explanations about how to resolve the doubt concerning whether substance can be spoken of as a relative, about the ways in which "prior" may be said, or about why alteration differs from the other kinds of motions are consciously cast according to generally accepted or unexamined opinion, but he does admit at the very end of the treatise that his discussion of the different meanings of "to have" proceeded according to what is usually said. Aristotle does not, however, claim that he did so in order to facilitate instruction.

Even though Averroes' interpretation is without textual corroboration, it helps to explain particular as well as general problems. By distinguishing between a definition based on unexamined opinion and one which is true, or between what he calls an accidental description and a true one, Averroes is able to show that the logical relationship of "head" to "man" is only accidental and thus not a valid instance of relation in substance. At the same time, Aver-

---

[10] See below, paras. 1, 2, and 49, with 60-62, 103, 108-109, and 111-113; also Aristotle *Categories* 8ª13-35, 14ᵇ10-23, 15ª13-33, and 15ᵇ31-33.

roes' repeated emphasis on the non-technical aspects of Aristotle's arguments reminds the reader of the broader context surrounding the *Categories*. Precisely because it is an introductory account of the way thoughts are ordered and expressed in language, it must start from what is most obvious to those learning the art and from the ways in which they usually express themselves. Rather than set forth a series of definitions, Aristotle chose to start with what was familiar and to move gradually from the customary use of speech and from the unreflective expression of ideas to a more technical appreciation of these phenomena. After all, many people who have little or no critical awareness of how language functions nonetheless manage to express themselves quite adequately.

A corollary of Averroes' willingness to highlight Aristotle's reliance on generally accepted or unexamined opinion is his reluctance to explore at any length the way similar ideas are expressed differently in Greek and Arabic. Though he does speak to the issue when it is raised by Aristotle, he does not do so on his own initiative.[11] And this is appropriate, for such differences between Greek and Arabic take on significance only as the discussion centers more on expression than on thought. Here the emphasis is on what is common to all thinking human beings and thus to all languages.

That is because the inquiry is into speech about existing things or, differently stated, into the way they are denoted by what we say. Thus it is important to distinguish the kinds of names we use to denote them as well as to explain how the terms are actually used to speak about these existing things and about their attributes. In keeping with his understanding that Aristotle's procedure here is based on what is generally accepted, Averroes makes no attempt to explain why Aristotle subsumes existing things under homonymous, synonymous, and derived names—or nouns, the distinction being more a matter of usage than anything

[11] See below, para. 78 and notes 41-42, with Aristotle *Categories* 10ᵃ28-10ᵇ12.

else—nor does he step aside to explain other instances of Aristotle's terminology. Instead he fills out and slightly rearranges Aristotle's account in order to bring out its salient features without intruding upon the scene.[12] In part, his reticence seems to derive from his understanding that this section of the book serves as an introduction in which the principles and definitions to be used in the sequel are set down. Considering these definitions and principles to be sufficiently clear in themselves, he offers no further explanation. His reticence is also partly due to the fact that even though Aristotle does have recourse to technical terminology on occasion here—for example, his references to essence, quiddity, and differentia—the subsequent discussion depends in no way on a fastidious understanding of such terms.

Thus, by whatever terms we call them, there are some names (homonymous) that can be used to speak of two quite different entities without the precise definition of either one applying to the other, just as there are names (synonymous) that apply to two different entities insofar as they do share the same definition. A final kind of names (derived) points to a particular characteristic of some entity by using a different form of the name of that particular characteristic to stand for the entity. Without saying so explicitly, both Aristotle and Averroes present this group of names as exhaustive. Even though Averroes speaks of many more instances of names in his *Short Commentaries on Aristotle's Logic*, a careful consideration of the way he describes these other names—transferred, metaphorical, dissimilar, general, and specific—reveals that each can be subsumed under one of the three kinds mentioned in the *Categories*.[13] These names denote only one way in which existing things can be spoken about. In addition to naming them, one can speak about what they do or what they are

[12] See below, paras. 2, 3-6, 7-11, and 13, with Aristotle *Categories* 1ª1-19, 1ª20-1ᵇ9, and 1ᵇ16-24.

[13] See Averroes "Discussion of What Utterances Signify," paras. 4-7 in my forthcoming edition and translation of his *Short Commentaries on Aristotle's Logic*.

like. In this sense, names constitute one aspect of a larger whole; they are a species or a kind of speech, the larger whole or genus being speech itself. When speech is formulated, it comes forth as utterances.

Though it sounds strange today to speak of "utterances," since the term "words" has a more familiar ring, both Aristotle and Averroes avoid the latter term throughout this whole discussion. Since speech which is limited to pronouncing a series of uncombined utterances—such as "horse," "runs," "man," "animal"—communicates no ideas, it is necessary to consider how utterances can be combined. "The horse runs" or "man is an animal" are good examples of how utterances in combination express ideas. In both instances something is said of something else; or, to be more precise, in both instances a predicate is applied to a subject. Like Aristotle, Averroes distinguishes between subject and predicate in a given statement by means of two criteria— what is or is not in a subject and what is or is not said of a subject—which are variously combined so as to give four classifications: what is both in a subject and said of a subject, what is in a subject but not said of a subject, what is not in a subject but is said of a subject, and what is neither in a subject nor said of a subject. The first two account for general and individual instances of accident respectively, and the second two for general and individual instances of substance respectively. The examples Aristotle and Averroes give of general accident and substance show that they mean species and genera of each, whereas they take individual accident or substance to be a designated instance such as the whiteness in a given body or a certain individual. Though neither explains here why criteria grounded in the basic differences between subject and predicate, as well as between the general and the individual, are used to arrive at this kind of differentiation between substance and accident, a remark made elsewhere by Averroes is instructive. In his short commentary on this work, he explains that the ten categories actually consist of substance and nine accidents. The observation did not originate with him, and probably not even with Ibn Sīnā, who stated the same thing in his

Shifā, but it is nonetheless persuasive.[14] Quantity, quality, position, and being acted upon, to mention only a few instances of the categories, do, after all, account for such accidental features of different substances as how tall this man is, what color he is, whether or not he is standing, and whether or not he is being chilled by the wind.

Passing quickly over a statement of the conditions under which several things may be predicated of a single subject without giving rise to confusion, both Aristotle and Averroes turn to an enumeration of the categories. It is accompanied by one or two brief examples of each category, nothing more. That the discussion turns almost immediately thereafter to a lengthy account of four of the categories—substance, quantity, relation, and quality—is not a sufficient reason for such taciturnity here. For a fuller account of what the categories represent, it is necessary to look elsewhere. In the *Topics*, Aristotle explains at some length why the four basic predicates—definition, particular characteristic, genus, and accident—are always in one or more of these categories, an account Averroes reduces to the following formulation: "The things in which all of these predicates are found are the ten categories, because each of the categories has definitions, genera, particular characteristics, and accidents."[15] It seems, then, that the categories are, properly speaking, predicates and even predicates of predicates. They may also function as subjects under certain circumstances, but that is of less interest. Given a particular subject, as is inevitably the case, the problem centers on what can appropriately be said or predicated of the subject.

[14] See Averroes "Discussion of the Categories," para. 3 in *Short Commentaries on Aristotle's Logic*, and Ibn Sīnā *al-Shifā, al-Manṭiq: al-Maqūlāt*, ed. G. Anawati et al. (Cairo: GEBO, 1959), p. 6.

[15] See below, paras. 14-15 with Aristotle *Categories* 1ᵇ25-2ᵃ3. See also Averroes *Talkhīṣ Kitāb al-Jadal*, ed. C. Butterworth and A. Haridi (Cairo: GEBO, 1979), para. 20, with Aristotle *Topics* 103ᵇ20-104ᵃ2. For the discussion of this and the preceding paragraph, I have learned much from J. L. Ackrill's notes to his translation of Aristotle's *Categories*; see *Aristotle's Categories and De Interpretatione*, trans. J. L. Ackrill (Oxford: Clarendon Press, 1963), pp. 74-76 and 77-81.

Hereafter, Averroes' skill as a commentator becomes especially evident. His divisions of Aristotle's discussions of each of the categories and his summaries of those discussions in terms of his divisions make Aristotle's explanation more accessible. Similarly, his attempts to point out what is particularly characteristic of each category, though not without basis in Aristotle's text, are very helpful because they are so nuanced.[16] Moreover, Averroes' summary of Aristotle's chapters 10-15 at the very beginning of the commentary as making known "the general conditions and common accidents which pertain to all of the categories or to most of them, insofar as they are categories" provides a sound basis for thinking through the problem of why all of these additional topics are introduced after the main subject of the treatise has been explained.

In addition, Averroes explicitly injects his own opinion into the commentary at a number of places in order to clarify particular questions. Thus he appends to Aristotle's attempt to explain why quantity does not admit of contrariety a further distinction so that the reader will not take this argument as a proof for relation admitting contrariety. Similarly, he recapitulates a particularly involved discussion of the problems involved in finding balanced correlatives by noting that what Aristotle has just done is to provide a rule for finding the balanced connection. And when Aristotle sums up his discussion of the kind of qualities enumerated with respect to figure and shape, allowing that other qualities might exist which fit into this genus, Averroes explains at greater length that Aristotle seems to have been thinking about qualities which may arise from considering specific images of things rather than the qualities which pertain to images insofar as they are composed of matter. These various suggestions for a clearer reading of Aristotle's text more than compensate for his vexing silence

---

[16] See below, para. 18 with paras. 21, 27, and 30-32; para. 34 with paras. 41 and 47-48; para. 49 with paras. 53-55, 58, and 63; para. 65 with para. 81; and para. 88 with para. 101; also Aristotle *Categories* 2^a19-33, 3^a15-32, and 3^b25-4^b20; 5^b11-15 and 6^a20-35; 6^b28-7^a30; 7^b15-8^a12, and 8^a37-8^b21; 11^a15; and 14^a7-13.

about why the category "to have" is discussed in some detail at the very end of the *Categories* even though the account of the categories of substance, quantity, relation, and quality concluded with the declaration that no more needed to be said about "to have," since the examples given of it in the original enumeration of the categories were sufficient.[17]

The preceding are not the only instances of Averroes' altering his usual commentary in order to speak in his own name. He also does so in order to call attention to the history of commentary, correct or erroneous, about certain points as well as to alert the reader to other works by Aristotle in which a particular issue is discussed at greater length. For example, when trying to explain the difference between secondary substances—that is, species or genera—and accidents, Averroes criticizes both al-Fārābī and the commentators for failing to understand why the definition of an accident cannot possibly be predicated as the definition of the subject in which it exists. However, when commenting on Aristotle's argument that state and condition appear to fall under both the category of relation and that of quality only because of a failure to distinguish between their species and genera, Averroes acknowledges that he owes his understanding of this point to al-Fārābī. Elsewhere, he notes that the commentators' solution to the problem of whether or not correlatives exist simultaneously by nature, though manifestly correct, is cast in terms too sophisticated for the level of discussion in this treatise. Here, also, he argues that in this treatise Aristotle wishes to restrict the discussion to the level of what is generally accepted and points to the *Metaphysics* as the treatise in which Aristotle resolves the problem along the lines used by the commentators.[18]

---

[17] See below, para. 46 and para. 49 with para. 51; paras. 53-55 with para. 56; para. 76 with para. 77; and para. 87 with paras. 111-113; also Aristotle *Categories* 6ª11-19 and 6ᵇ15-19; 6ᵇ28-7ª30 and 7ª31-7ᵇ10; 10ª25-27; and 11ᵇ10-15 with 15ᵇ17-33.

[18] See below, paras. 21, 82-83, 58-59, and 39, with Aristotle *Categories* 2ª19-33, 11ª20-38, 7ᵇ15-8ª12, and 5ª15-37.

IV

In sum, Averroes' *Middle Commentary on Aristotle's Categories* is an intelligent, instructive guide to Aristotle's teaching in this work. His detailed explanation of the order of the argument helps the reader discern the steps in Aristotle's otherwise obscure exposition. His interpretation that the work is based on generally received opinions, coupled with his indications about how Aristotle discusses some of the issues presented here much more thoroughly in other works, permit the reader to gain new insight into Aristotle's writing style and into the larger question of the relationship between style per se and philosophic inquiry. And his painstaking explanation of Aristotle's account of substance, quantity, relation, and quality, as well as of his account of opposites, prior and posterior, simultaneous, motion, and "to have," alert the reader to the basic teaching and to its nuances. Without such a commentary, it would be extremely difficult to understand Aristotle's treatise.

There are, however, a number of questions that are not resolved by Averroes. His own habit of adhering closely to Aristotle's text keeps him, for example, from explaining precisely what categories are as well as why they seem to break down into substance plus nine accidents. Though categories do seem to be predicates or predicates of predicates, why is this so and what does it mean? To discern that in Greek the term "category" comes from the same root as "predicate" is no more helpful than to recognize that in Arabic it has the literal sense of "what is said of" something else, for in either case one must ask the further question of why that linguistic formulation was chosen in the first place. And a fuller explanation of why the categories when, where, doing and being acted upon, and even position deserve a less complete investigation here would have permitted one to understand them and their relationship to the other categories better. At the same time, Averroes could have helped the reader immensely by explaining why it is proper to begin to study the art of logic by means of this work, but why it is nonetheless so difficult.

Such lacunae detract from what is otherwise a very thoughtful explanation of Aristotle's treatise. To the extent that Averroes' failure to address himself to such questions is part of his decision to be a faithful exegete of Aristotle rather than to use the commentary format to introduce his own ideas, one can criticize him for his lack of originality. But, as should be evident by now, the original question of whether Averroes differs in any marked fashion from Aristotle or whether his commentary contains anything new proposes a woefully inadequate criterion by which to judge the merits of this work.

THE ORDER OF THE ARGUMENT

Chapter Five:
Quantity has no contrary at all (para. 41)
Few and many, big and small are relations (para. 42)
Big and small are not contraries (para. 43)
Contraries cannot come together in one subject (para. 44)
Big and small, few and many are not contraries (para. 45)
Quantity is a contrary only insofar as it is place (para. 46)
Chapter Six: Quantity does not admit of the lesser and the greater (para. 47)
Chapter Seven: Equal and unequal are most particularly characteristic of quantity (para. 48)
Section Three—About the Category of Relation:
The chapters of Section Three (para. 49)
Chapter One: A general description of relative things and examples of them (para. 50)
Chapter Two: Relative things admit of contraries (para. 51)
Chapter Three: Some relatives admit of the lesser and the greater (para. 52)
Chapter Four:
The particular characteristic of each relative is that it reciprocates with the other (para. 53)
The relation of correlatives and non-correlatives (para. 54)
How to make a relation for things which do not have a name indicating a relation (para. 55)
Chapter Five:
The rule for selecting the attribute which has the balanced connection (para. 56)
How to infer this attribute (para. 57)
Chapter Six:
A doubt about whether it is a particular characteristic of relative things that they exist simultaneously by nature (para. 58)
How the commentators solved this doubt (para. 59)

Chapter Seven:
A doubt about whether relation can exist in substances (para. 60)
How Aristotle solves this doubt (para. 61)
Averroes' interpretation of Aristotle's solution (para. 62)
Chapter Eight:
One particular characteristic of relative terms is that when one of them is definitely known, the other is necessarily known (para. 63)
Difficulty of judging what is relative (para. 64)
Section Four—The Discussion of Quality:
The chapters of Section Four (para. 65)
Chapter One: Definition of quality (para. 66)
Chapter Two:
The first kind: state and condition (para. 67)
What the name state signifies in Greek (para. 68)
Chapter Three: The second kind: what does or does not have a natural faculty (para. 69)
Chapter Four:
The third kind: affective qualities and affections (para. 70)
Why some of these are said to be affective qualities (para. 71)
Why colors are said to be affective qualities or affections (para. 72)
Affective qualities and affections taken from the accidents of the soul (para. 73)
Chapter Five: The fourth kind: figure and shape and straightness and crookedness (para. 74)
Chapter Six:
Whether sparse, dense, rough, and smooth fall under the fourth kind or under position (para. 75)
Aristotle's denial that qualities other than those enumerated exist (para. 76)
Averroes' interpretation of this (para. 77)
Chapter Seven: Derived names are used to designate things described as qualities (para. 78)

THE TEXT

1. The most illustrious jurist, the accomplished scholar, Abū al-Walīd ibn Rushd, may God be pleased with him, said: the purpose of this discussion is to comment[1] upon the ideas[2] contained in Aristotle's books on the art of logic and to study them insofar as we are able, as has been our custom with the rest of his books. We will begin with the first of his books on this art, which is the *Categories*. Thus, we say that in general this book is divided into three parts.

The first part is on the order of an introduction to what he wants to say in this book. That is because it contains the matters which, with respect to what he wants to say in this book, perform the same function as principles which are set down and as definitions.

In the second part, he mentions the ten categories, category by category, and provides for each one the description particular to it. And he divides them into their generally accepted species and gives their generally accepted particular characteristics.

In the third part, he makes known the general corollaries and common accidents which pertain to all of the categories or to most of them, insofar as they are categories.

[1] Literally, "make a middle commentary" (*talkhīṣ*).

[2] Or "meanings" (*ma'ānī*). The term *ma'nā* (plural, *ma'ānī*) can be translated in a number of different ways: idea, notion, thought, meaning, thing, and signification—to name a few.

Part One

2. There are five chapters in this part.

In the first, he indicates the conditions pertaining to beings insofar as they are denoted by utterances.

In the second, he indicates what substance and accident are as they are investigated in this art, I mean, universal and individual substance and universal and individual accident.

In the third, he makes it known that when a predicate is so predicated of a subject as to make its substance known and another predicate is predicated of that predicate so as to make its substance known, that subsequent predicate also makes the substance of the first subject known.

In the fourth, he indicates which genera can share divisible differentiae and which cannot.

In the fifth, he sets about dividing uncombined beings into the ten categories by means of examples and he makes it known that affirmation and negation do not apply to the uncombined beings which are denoted by uncombined utterances but only to combined beings insofar as they are denoted by utterances in combination.

CHAPTER ONE

1ª1-5   3. He said: things having homonymous—that is, shared—names are things which have not a single thing in common and shared, except for the name alone. The definition of each one which makes its substance understood according to the way it is denoted by that shared name is different from the definition of the other one and is particular to what it defines. An example of that is the name "animal" said of a depicted man and of a rational man. For the definitions of both

of these are different and have nothing in common
and shared, except for the name alone—which is our
saying "animal" with respect to both of them.

4. Things having synonymous names are those whose   1ᵃ6-12
name is both precisely the same and shared, and the
definition setting forth their substance according to
what is denoted by that name is also precisely the same.
An example of that is the name "animal" said of a man
and of a horse. For the name "animal" is common to
both of them and denotes a single substance with respect to both of them—namely, our saying "a self-nourishing, sensing body," which is the definition of animal.

5. Those having derived names are those which are   1ᵃ13-15
called by the name of an idea[1] existing in them. However, their names have an inflection different from the
name of that idea due to their encompassing the subject of that idea as well as the idea, like calling someone
"courageous" from the name "courage" and "eloquent" from the name "eloquence."

6. Of the ideas denoted by utterances, some are un-   1ᵃ16-19
combined and are denoted by uncombined utter-
ances—like "man" and "horse." And some are combined and are denoted by utterances in combination—
like our saying "man is an animal" and "the horse runs."

CHAPTER TWO

7. He said: some beings are predicated of a subject   1ᵃ20-22
and are not in a subject. That is, some make known
the substance and quiddity of everything of which they
are predicated and in no way make anything external
to the substance of a subject known. This is the general[2]
substance, like animal and man. For if they are both

---

[1] This is a literal translation of the term *ism maʿnā;* it may also be
translated as "abstract noun"; see W. Wright, *A Grammar of the Arabic
Language* (Cambridge: Cambridge University Press, 1962), vol. 1, p.
107B.

[2] This is the same word (*ʿāmm*) which has previously been translated as "common," but here, and again in paras. 9 and 11, Averroes
uses this term as a synonym for "universal" (*kullīy*); see para. 2,
description of Chapter Two.

predicated of something, they make known its substance and essence—nothing external to its essence.

1ª23-28   8. Some are in a subject—that is, not a part of it—
and cannot be constituted apart from a subject nor be
in any way predicated of a subject—that is, by way of
what it is.[3] This is the designated individual accident—
like this designated blackness and this designated
whiteness existing in this designated body, since every
color is in a body.

1ª29-1ᵇ2   9. Some are predicated of a subject and are also in
a subject—that is, predicated of two things and making
the quiddity of one of the two known but not that of
the other one insofar as it is a part of the substance of
the one whose quiddity it makes known and not a part
of the substance of the one whose quiddity it does not
make known, but is constituted by the subject. This is
the general[4] accident—like our predicating knowledge
of the soul and of writing, for we say "writing is knowledge" and "knowledge is in the soul." So, when we
predicate it of writing, it makes its substance known,
since it is its genus and may appropriately be given in
response to "what is writing?" When it is predicated of
the soul and it is said "in the soul there is knowledge,"
it makes known something external to the soul's essence.

1ᵇ2-5   10. Some are neither predicated of a subject—that
is, as predicates that make its substance known—nor
in a subject—that is, predicated of a subject so as to
make anything external to its substance known. And
this is the designated individual substance, like Zayd
and ʿAmr. It is not predicated of anything in a natural
manner, neither as a predicate which makes the substance of the subject known nor as a predicate that
does not make it known.

1ᵇ6-9   11. On the whole, substance, whether it be general[5]

---

[3] This is a literal translation of *min ṭarīq mā huwa*. The substantive
of *mā huwa* is rendered as "quiddity" (*māhīyah*).

[4] See para. 7, note 2.

[5] See para. 7, note 2.

or individual, is that which is not in a subject at all. And on the whole, accident, whether it be general[5] or individual, is that which is in a subject. And on the whole, the general,[5] whether it be a substance or an accident, is that which is said of a subject. On the whole, the individual, whether it be an accident or a substance, is that which is not said of a subject. Thus universal substance is distinguished from individual substance in that universal substance is said of a subject and individual substance is not. And individual accident is distinguished from universal accident in that universal accident is said of a subject and individual accident is not.

CHAPTER THREE

12. He said: when something is so predicated of a   1ᵇ10-15
subject as to make its substance known and then another predicate is so predicated of that predicate as to make its substance known as well, it also makes known the substance of the subject which the first predicate made known. For example, when "man" is predicated of Zayd and ʿAmr it makes their substance known. And when a second predicate is predicated of man so as to make his substance known—like "animal"—it necessarily follows that it makes known the substance of Zayd and ʿAmr which "man" made known.

CHAPTER FOUR

13. He said: genera which are different and are not   1ᵇ16-24
ranked under one another—that is, which are not subordinate to one another—have differentiae which differ in kind. For example, the differentiae into which animal is divided—like "walking," "flying," and "swimming"—are other than the differentiae into which knowledge is divided. For animal is subordinate to the genus of substance, whereas knowledge is subordinate to the genus of quality. And quality and substance are two ultimate genera which are not subordinate to one

another. Nothing prevents one from supposing that
the differentiae of the genera which are subordinate
to one another are similar in kind. For example, "animal" is divided into "aquatic" and "terrestial" just as
the "self-nourishing" is, and "animal" is ranked under
"self-nourishing." The reason for that is that the differentiae into which the ultimate genus is divided are
undoubtedly predicated of genera which are subordinate to the ultimate genus, for it is predicated of
every one of those genera subordinate to it. So when
those differentiae into which the ultimate genus is divided do not constitute the genera subordinate to it,
those genera are divided into them as is the ultimate
genus. For when they are predicated and are not con-
stitutive, they are co-ordinate.

CHAPTER FIVE

1ᵇ25-28   14. He said: uncombined utterances which denote
uncombined ideas necessarily denote one of ten things—
either substance, or quantity, or quality, or relation, or
where, or when, or position, or to have, or doing, or
being acted upon.

1ᵇ29-2ᵃ3   15. So, by way of example, substance is like man or
horse. Quantity is like your saying "two cubits" and
"three cubits." Quality is like your saying "white" and
"writing." Relation is like double and half. Where is
like your saying "Zayd is in the house." When is like
your saying "a year ago" or "yesterday." Position is like
to be reclining and to be sitting. To have is like your
saying "shod" and "armed." Doing is like your saying
"burning" and "cutting." Being acted upon is like your
saying "being burned" and "being cut."

2ᵃ4-10   16. When each one of these ten is taken singly,[6] it
is not denoted by an affirmation or a negation. When
some are combined with others, then the affirmative
and negative occur—like your saying "this is a quantity," "this is not a quantity." And when the affirmative

---

[6] That is, "uncombined" (*mufradatan*).

and negative occur, truth and falsehood enter. For with uncombined ideas—like our saying "man" in isolation or "white" in isolation—truth and falsehood do not enter. However, when they are combined and it is said "man is white," it is possible for this statement to be true and for it to be false. For with combination, both things occur—I mean, affirmation and negation and truth and falsehood.

PART TWO

17. This part is divided into six sections.

In the first section, he mentions the category of substance.

In the second, the category of quantity.

In the third, the category of relation.

In the fourth, the category of quality.

In the fifth, the category of doing and of being acted upon.

In the sixth, the categories of position, and time,[1] and place,[2] and to have.

SECTION ONE

18. There are fourteen chapters in this section.

In the first, he makes it known that there are two sorts of substance—primary and secondary—and he tells about each one of them.

In the second, he makes known what the secondary substances are.

In the third, he makes it known that the particular characteristic of secondary substances—these being the ones which are said of a subject—is that their name and definition are predicated of their subject and that it is not like this with those things which are said to be[3] in a subject—these being the accidents.

In the fourth, he makes it known that everything but primary substances has need of the primary substances to exist.

In the fifth, he makes it known that the species of

[1] Literally, "when" (*matā*).
[2] Literally, "where" (*ayn*).
[3] The words "things" and "to be" have been added for clarity.

the secondary substances is more properly substance than the genus, and that the primary substances—these being the individual substances—are more properly so than the species, and that the reason for this—I mean, that the name substance is more appropriate for the individual than for the species and for the species than for the genus—is similar.

In the sixth, he makes it known that with the secondary substances which are of the same order, none is more properly substance than another, and it is similar with the primary substances.

In the seventh, he makes known the way in which the species and genera found in these categories deserve to be called secondary substances—these being the ones predicated of a subject to the exclusion of the ones predicated in a subject, which are the accidents— and the way in which the individuals deserve to be called primary substances.

In the eighth, he describes substance taken in an absolute sense, whether it be individual or universal. And in it, he sets forth the particular characteristics which distinguish secondary substances from accident taken in an absolute sense.

In the ninth, he makes it known that the differentiae share these particular characteristics which distinguish secondary substances from accidents.

In the tenth, he makes it known that all of the secondary substances and differentiae pertain to things that have synonymous names.

In the eleventh, he removes the ambiguity which leads to secondary substances being confused with primary and being imagined as one in kind.

In the twelfth, he makes it known that a particular characteristic of this category is that it has no contrary and that this is a particular characteristic other categories may share.

In the thirteenth, he makes it known that a particular characteristic of this category is that it admits of neither the lesser nor the greater, whereas the rest of the categories do admit of them.

In the fourteenth, he makes it known that the particular characteristic most proper to the category of substance is that it admits of contrary qualifications, offers proofs of that, and resolves an ambiguity occurring with respect to it.

CHAPTER ONE: THE DISCUSSION OF SUBSTANCE

2ª11-13   19. He said: substances are of two sorts, primary and secondary. The substance characterized as being primary—which is the one said to be substance in a correct and prior sense—is the individual substance whose general description was given earlier—I mean, the one which is neither said of a subject nor is in a subject, like this designated man and this designated horse.[4]

CHAPTER TWO

2ª14-18   20. The ones said to be secondary substances are the species in which the individual substances, as well as the genera of these species, exist in a manner similar to that of the part existing in the whole. For example, this designated Zayd is in the species—that is, in man—and man is in the genus, which is animal. So this designated Zayd is primary substance, and man and animal that are predicated of him are both secondary substances.

CHAPTER THREE

2ª19-33   21. It is clear from what was said in the introduction to this book that those which are said of a subject—namely, the secondary substances—must necessarily have their name and definition predicated of that subject.[5] For example, the name "man" applies to[6] this

---

[4] See above, para. 10.
[5] See above, paras. 7 and 12.
[6] Or "is true of" (*yaṣduq ʿalā*).

designated Zayd and so does its definition, for we say of Zayd that he is a man and we say of him that he is a rational animal, which is the definition of man. Now those said in a subject—namely, the accidents—for the most part[7] furnish the subject neither its name nor its definition. When we say Zayd is white, for example, and in saying "white" denote a quality in Zayd—which is its dominant sense—white is neither a name nor a definition for Zayd. When we use a derived name to denote the subject of the quality so as to make it known, it may be its name, and we would then say that the predicate furnishes the name of the subject. But that

[7] The passage from here to the end of the paragraph exists in the Florence manuscript and in all of the other manuscripts except Leiden. Contrary to the understanding I had of the text when I was preparing the Arabic edition, I now think that the following passage, which is absent from both the Florence and Dublin manuscripts, ought to be read as a variant:

‹ " . . . have neither their name nor their definition predicated of the designated subject. Whiteness, for example, is not predicated of body so that it is said 'body is whiteness'; nor is its definition predicated so that it is said 'body is a color which pierces vision.' With some subjects it may happen that the name is predicated without the definition—like our saying in Arabic 'a dirham is a mintage of the ruler,' for the definition of mintage is not predicated of dirham. If they are denoted by derived names, their name and definition may apply to the subject. However, the definition is not predicated of the subject so as to make its substance known, the way the definitions of substances are predicated of substances. For example, white is in a subject—that is, in body—and it may be attributed to body and predicated of it, so that it is said that it is white. Yet the definition of white is in no way predicated of body insofar as it makes its substance known."

The definition of white as "a color which pierces vision" could also be rendered "a color which dilates vision," the verb being *yufarriq*. In the *Metaphysics* X.vii.7.1057ᵇ8-9, Aristotle defines the color white as that which penetrates or dilates vision, whereas black is that which compresses or obscures it. When explaining this definition in his *Long Commentary on Aristotle's Metaphysics*, Averroes uses an expression almost identical to the one occurring here; see *Tafsīr Mā Baʿd al-Ṭabīʿah*, ed. M. Bouyges (Beirut: Imprimerie Catholique, 1973), vol. III, p. 1357. See also Aristotle *Topics* III.v.119ᵃ31-32 and Plato *Timaeus* 67D-E.

is not in any way possible with the definition, for the definition of whiteness cannot possibly be the definition of Zayd. This is the true interpretation of this chapter, not what Abū Naṣr [al-Fārābī] supposed, which I suppose he reported the commentators as saying.

CHAPTER FOUR

2ª34-2ᵇ6   22. Everything other than primary substances, which are individuals, is either said of a subject or in a subject. And that is evident from scrutiny and induction—I mean, the need both kinds have for a subject. For example, it is correct to predicate life of man because it applies to a designated man. So if it did not apply to any one individual person, it would not be correct to predicate it of man, which is the species. Similarly, it is correct to predicate color of body because of its existence in a certain designated body.[8] It follows necessarily, then, that anything other than primary substances is either said of them or in them—that is, of primary substances or in them. And if that is so, then if primary substances did not exist, there would be no way for secondary substances or for accidents to exist.

CHAPTER FIVE

2ᵇ7-22   23. The species of secondary substances are more appropriately called substances than the genera, because they are closer than the genera to the primary substances. That is because when either of the two is used in response to "what is the individual"—that is, the primary substance—it is a response consistent with the question "what is it." Yet responding to the question "what is it" in terms of the species makes the designated individual more completely known and is more consistent than responding in terms of the genus. For example, if a respondent responds to the question "what

---

[8] The verb *yaṣduq* and its substantives have been rendered as "is correct" and "apply" in this and the two preceding sentences. See para. 21, note 6.

is Socrates" with "he is a man," this makes Socrates more completely known than responding "he is an animal." For humanity is more a particular characteristic of Socrates than animality, and this is like the more general with respect to the more particular. This, then, is one consideration which shows that the species are more deserving of the name substantiality than the genera. There is another indication as well. It is that primary substances are surely more deserving of the name substance and of the name existent being[9] than secondary substances and accidents, because all other things are either predicated of them or in them. And with respect to the species, the genera are in the same situation as all things with respect to the primary substances—I mean that the primary substances are subjects for all other things, just as the species are subjects for the genera. The genera, then, are predicated of the species, just as all other things are predicated of the primary substances.[10] The converse—that the species are to be predicated of the genera—does not hold any more than it holds with respect to all other things being predicated of the primary substances—I mean, that the primary[11] substances are not predicated of them. This being so, the species must necessarily be more deserving of the name substance than the genera.

CHAPTER SIX

24. Of the species of substances which are not genera, none is more deserving of the name substance than another. For your response with respect to Zayd that he is a man provides no more knowledge than your response with respect to this designated horse

2ᵇ23-29

---

[9] Or, more literally, "that which exists" (*al-mawjūd*).

[10] In the Arabic, this sentence and the two preceding ones form one long conditional sentence with the apodosis coming at the beginning of this sentence. Even though the term "primary" in this last prepositional phrase seems to be required by the larger argument, it is not present in the Arabic.

[11] Here, too, the term "primary" is missing from the Arabic.

that it is a horse. Similarly, no primary substance is more deserving of the name substantiality than another. For this designated man is no more deserving of the name substantiality than this designated horse.

CHAPTER SEVEN

2ᵇ30-3ᵃ6   25. Of all the things predicated of primary substances, it is only their species and genera that are called secondary substances. For when one of them is used in response to "what is the primary substance," it makes it known—even though responding with the species makes it better known. When something other than these is used in response to that, the response is neither appropriate nor adequate to the question. For example, if in response to "what is Zayd," a man responds "he is a man," this provides more knowledge than "he is a living being"—even though both of them make his quiddity known. If he were to respond "he is white" or "he is two cubits tall," he would respond in terms of something foreign to him and something external to his nature. Thus, as distinct from the rest of the other categories, these have necessarily been called secondary substances. This is one of the things that makes it evident why, as distinct from the rest of the things predicated of them, only the species and genera of the primary substances have been particularly characterized by the name substance. This may also become evident in the following way: namely, that the primary substances stand in the same analogous relationship to the rest of things as the species and genera of substances to the rest of the universals of the other categories. That is because just as all the rest of the things either are predicated of primary substances or exist in them—as we have said—so, too, all the rest of the universals of the categories exist in secondary substances—I mean, that their universals exist in the universals of the secondary substances just as their individual instances exist in the individual instances of the primary substances.[12] For example, grammar exists in man and being two cubits tall in body.

CHAPTER EIGHT

26. Common to every substance, whether it be in-   3ᵃ7-9
dividual or universal, is that it does not exist in a subject. That is because there are two sorts of substances—primary and secondary. Primary substances, as has been said, are neither in a subject nor of a subject.[13] On the other hand, secondary substances are of a subject, not in a subject. Thus what is common to both sorts is that they are not in a subject.

CHAPTER NINE

27. We have already said that what particularly char-   3ᵃ15-32
acterizes secondary substances is that they are said of a subject but not in a subject, that their name and definition may therefore be predicated of the subject insofar as they are said of the subject, and that of those things which are in a subject the name of some may happen to be said of the subject but not their definition.[14] However, this is nothing particularly characteristic of secondary substances, for the differentia is also said of a subject but not in a subject. An example of that is being rational. It is predicated of man, not in him, since it does not exist in him the way whiteness does in body. Therefore, the name and definition of the differentia may also be true of the subject, as occurs with the secondary substances. For being rational and its definition—namely, apprehending by means of thought and deliberation—are predicated of man by

---

[12] See above, paras. 22 and 23.
[13] See above, para. 19 and also para. 10.
[14] See above, para. 21. The word "things" has been added here to avoid confusion; as was explained in para. 21 as well as in paras. 8, 9, and 11, only accidents are in a subject.

way of what he is.[15] Nor can anyone confute us by saying that reason and differentiae in general exist in a subject—that is, in the things of which they are differentiae—just as accidents exist in a subject—the one like reason existing in man and the other like whiteness existing in body. For reason exists in a subject—I mean, in man—only in that it is part of him, and the case is not the same with respect to whiteness and body. Therefore it ought not to be inferred from our statement regarding the general description of accidents as things said in a subject that they are like a part of it, but rather that the subject exists without respect to them.[16]

CHAPTER TEN

3ª33-3ᵇ9   28. What is particularly characteristic of secondary substances and of differentiae is that whenever they are predicated, they are predicated in the same way as things having synonymous names. That is because whenever they are predicated, they are predicated either of individuals or of species. For primary substances are predicated of nothing at all. The species is predicated of the individual, like man of Zayd. And genera are predicated of species and of individuals. The definitions of the species and genera of the primary substances must, then, necessarily be predicated of them, just as their names are predicated of them. That is evident with respect to their species. And with respect to their genera, it is evident from what has preceded. That is because the genus is said of the species and the species of the primary substance, namely, the individual. It has already been stated that everything said of the predicate which is said of a subject is also said of that subject. And this is the situation of the genus with respect to the species and the individual.[17] Similarly,

[15] Or "essentially" (*'alā ṭarīq mā huwa*); see above, para. 8, note 3.
[16] See above, para. 11 and paras. 8-9.
[17] See above, para. 12.

the definitions of the differentiae are predicated of the individuals and the species in the same way as names are. If this is the case and it has already been said that things whose names are synonymous are those whose name and definition are common and precisely the same, then it follows that it must be a particular characteristic of the differentiae and of things in this category for them to be predicated of everything of which they are predicated in the way things having synonymous names are predicated.[18]

CHAPTER ELEVEN

29. It may be supposed that every substance signifies 3ᵇ10-24 only a designated substance, namely, the individual. Now with respect to primary substances it is clear that they do signify designated individuals, because what is inferred about them from their names is something which is numerically one. And with respect to secondary substances, it may be conjectured that because the names which signify them are similar to the names of individuals or because they are used in place of the names of individuals they signify a designated individual. But that is not the case. Instead, because the subject of that name is not precisely the same, as is the name which by its form signifies primary substance, it signifies any designated thing which happens along. That is, Zayd and ʿAmr signify only a designated thing, whereas man and animal and species and genus in general signify many things. In addition, they distinguish these things from others not in just a token manner, the way white distinguishes the thing to which it is attributed, but according to the substance of the thing. Species and genus are set down so as to set the thing apart from anything else with respect to substance, except that genus is more inclusive than species. That is, the name animal includes what the name man signifies, since animal is the genus of man.

[18] See above, para. 4.

CHAPTER TWELVE

3ᵇ25-33   30. What is particularly characteristic of the category of substance is that it has no contrary, for there is no contrary of man or of animal. However, this particular characteristic is one other categories may share. An example of this is quantity, for there is no contrary to being two or ten cubits tall or to anything of this sort unless you say that few is contrary to many and that big is contrary to small. Yet it is clear that the species of discrete quantity—like five, three, and four—are not contrary to one another.

CHAPTER THIRTEEN

3ᵇ34-4ᵃ9   31. What is particularly characteristic of substance is that it does not admit of the lesser and the greater. I do not mean that one substance is not more deserving of the name substance than another, for that is something we postulated when we said that the individual substances are more properly substances than the universal ones. But what I do mean is that neither the species nor the genus of substances can be predicated of one individual more than of another, nor can either be predicated at one moment more than at another. For Zayd is no more an animal than ʿAmr, nor is Zayd more an animal today than he will be tomorrow.¹⁹ Yet this white thing can be whiter than this other white thing, and it can be whiter today than it was yesterday.

CHAPTER FOURTEEN

4ᵃ10-4ᵇ20   32. It may be supposed that what is most particularly characteristic of substance is that what is numerically one itself admits of contrary qualifications. That becomes clear through induction, for it is not possible that any numerically designated thing other than substance would admit of contrary qualifications. For no numerically one color exists which admits of white and

¹⁹ See above, paras. 18 and 23.

black, nor does the single self-same deed admit of praise
and blame. The same holds for all of the other categories which are not substance. With substances, the
single self-same thing admits of contrary qualifications.
For example, this designated Zayd is sometimes good
and at other times bad, sometimes hot and at other
times cold. Now there may be a certain doubt attached
to this induction with respect to speech and supposition. That is, it may be supposed that they both admit
of contraries. That is because the statement or supposition that Zayd is standing is true when Zayd is
standing and false when he is sitting. Thus, a single
self-same statement may itself admit of truth and falsehood, and these are contraries. Now if one grants that
this is what constitutes the admission of contraries, there
is still a difference between the two statements. That
is because the substance which admits of contraries
does so insofar as it is itself altered and rejects one of
the contraries while accepting the other. On the other
hand, the statement and supposition do not admit truth
and falsehood insofar as they are themselves altered,
but insofar as the thing to which the supposition refers
outside the mind is itself altered. For example, the
supposition that Zayd is sitting is indeed true[20] when
Zayd sits and false when he stands. Thus, if we grant
that this constitutes the admission of contrary qualities,
then the particular characteristic of substance is that
it is that which admits of contrary qualities insofar as
it is itself altered. It would be more proper for us to
say that this is not what constitutes the admission of
contraries. That is because when the statement and
supposition are described as true at one time and false
at another, they are not so described in the sense that
truth is something that itself arises in them at one moment and falsehood at another the way whiteness itself
arises in Zayd at one moment and blackness at another.
So truth and falsehood with respect to the statement

---

[20] Literally, "does admit of truth" (*innamā yaqbal al-ṣidq*).

are a certain relation and connection in keeping with the alteration in the thing about which there is a supposition and a statement, not anything itself arising. If this, then, is the case, the particular characteristic of substance must necessarily be such that what is numerically one admits of contrary qualities.

33. This is the extent of what he said about substance.

SECTION TWO

THE DISCUSSION OF QUANTITY

34. What he says about this category consists of seven chapters.

In the first, he makes known the major differentiae of quantity, that they are discreteness, continuity, position, and lack of position.

In the second, he makes known which generally accepted genera of quantity fall under discreteness and which fall under continuity.

In the third, he makes known which of these genera also fall under position and which do not.

In the fourth, he makes it known that the seven genera of quantity which were enumerated are the generally accepted genera which are essentially quantity and that whatever else is supposed to be quantity—like movement, lightness, and heaviness—is something which attaches to it by dint of existing in these genera.

In the fifth, he makes it known that one of the particular characteristics of quantity as well is to have no contrary. And he resolves the doubts because of which it is supposed that it does have contraries.

In the sixth, he makes it known that one of the particular characteristics of quantity as well is not to admit of the lesser and greater, as is the case with substance.

In the seventh, he makes it known that the true particular characteristic of quantity which nothing else has in common with it is equality and inequality.

CHAPTER ONE

35. He said: quantity is either discrete or continuous,   4ᵇ20-22
or it is such that some of its parts either have position
with respect to other parts or do not have position.

CHAPTER TWO

36. Discrete quantity is two-fold: number and speech.   4ᵇ23-24
Continuous quantity is five-fold: line, surface, body,
and what enfolds and encompasses bodies—namely,
time and place.

37. Number belongs to discrete quantity, because   4ᵇ25-38
discrete quantity is that for which it is impossible to
take a common term by means of which its parts are
continuous with each other. For example, there is no
common term by means of which one part of ten—
namely, five—is continuous with the five which is its
other part, nor the three in it continuous with the
seven. Instead, all of its parts are discrete from each
other. Now it is evident in the case of speech that it is
quantity because it is measured in terms of one of its
parts, that is, the smallest part which may be uttered—
either as in a long syllable, like *lā*, or as in a short one,
like *la*. It is discrete, too, since there is no common
term by means of which some of its parts are joined
with others. That is because syllables are discrete from
one another.

38. Now line, surface, body, time, and place are con-   5ᵃ1-14
tinuous quantity because for each one there can exist
a common term or terms by means of which some of
its parts are joined with others. This term is the point
with respect to the line, the line with respect to the
surface, the surface with respect to body, and the instant with respect to time. That is because the parts of
the line are continuous by means of the point, the parts
of the surface are continuous by means of the line, the
parts of body are continuous by means of the plane,²¹

²¹ Here and in the next paragraph, Averroes uses the term "plane"
(*saṭh*) interchangeably with the term "surface" (*basīṭ*).

and the two parts of time—namely, past and future—
are continuous by means of the instant. Now since the
parts of body occupy place and are continuous by means
of a common term, the parts of place must also be
continuous by means of a common term. And if this
is the case, then it must be continuous quantity.

CHAPTER THREE

5ª15-37   39. Now quantity constituted of parts some of which
have position with respect to others consists of line,
plane,[22] body, and place. The significance of some parts
having position with respect to others is that all of the
parts exist at the same time, for if they did not exist
at the same time, one part would not have a position
with respect to another; and that whichever part you
take you will find it to have a delimited position in that
quantity—either above or below—and to be continuous
with another delimited part. For example, the parts of
the line exist at the same time, each one of them in a
delimited manner and continuous with a delimited
part—namely, the part which follows it. The case is
the same with the parts of the plane,[22] the parts of
body, and the parts of place. For the parts of place
exist in the same way as do the parts of body which
occupy place, whether place is vacuum or the plane[22]
externally surrounded by body as Aristotle opines.[23]
Now with number we find not a single one of these
three conditions with respect to its parts, to say nothing
of them joining together in it—I mean, for them to
exist at the same time, for each one of them to exist
in a delimited manner, and to be continuous with a
delimited part. The case is the same with time and
speech—I mean, that their parts do not exist together,
since the parts of time and the parts of speech have
no constancy nor is one of the subsequent parts joined
to a preceding one. Instead, the parts of number and

[22] See preceding note.
[23] See Aristotle *Physics* IV.iv.211ª24-34 and 211ᵇ6-212ª7.

the parts of time have a particular order. For some time is prior and some subsequent. The same holds with number, for two is before three. But it certainly has no position.

CHAPTER FOUR

40. These primary genera of quantity are the ones which are truly and primarily quantity. Anything other than them ascribed to quantity is only accidentally and secondarily said to be quantity—I mean, by means of one of these which we said were truly quantity. For example, we say that this designated whiteness is large because it is in a large surface. Similarly, we say that the task is long because of it taking a long time. This becomes evident when someone asks "how extensive is this task,"[24] for the answer to that would be "it is a year-long task." And if he were to ask "how long is this white thing," it would be said "three or four cubits long." So the task is limited and measured in terms of time, and the white thing is measured in terms of the scope of the plane—which is three or four cubits long. If they were quantities essentially, they would be measured in terms of themselves.

$5^a38\text{-}5^b10$

CHAPTER FIVE

41. One of the particular characteristics of quantity is that it has no contraries at all, regardless of whether it is continuous or discrete quantity. For neither five nor three has a contrary, nor does the line or the plane. There are two reasons why no one should object that many and few belong to discrete quantity and are both contraries or, similarly, that big and small belong to continuous quantity and are both contraries.

$5^b11\text{-}15$

42. One is that neither few and many nor big and

$5^b16\text{-}22$

[24] Literally, "how much is this task," the interrogatory *kam* admitting of many translations. In the example which follows immediately, the interrogatory *kam* is likewise translated in a manner consistent with English usage.

small belong to quantity but to relation. That is because quantity exists essentially, whereas big and small and few and many are spoken of in reference to something else.[25] Therefore it is possible for a single self-same thing to be big and small and few and many, big in relation to one thing and small in relation to another—to the point that we might speak of a mountain as small and of a fish as big, despite the smallness of the fish and the greatness of the mountain. If the thing were small or big in itself and this were an attribute inhering in it essentially—like the whiteness which inheres in body—smallness would in no case be attributed to the mountain or bigness to the fish. This is one of the reasons for it becoming evident that quantity has no contrary—I mean, because these two belong to a category other than the category of quantity.

5ᵇ27-33   43. And it becomes evident that big and small are not contraries, whether we postulate them in the category of quantity or not, because there can be nothing contrary to that which is not intellectually apprehended in itself but is intellectually apprehended in reference to something else. That is because things contrary to each other are such that the existence of each is extremely distant from that of the other, whereas there is nothing which is extremely distant from anything spoken of in reference to something else since it is spoken of in reference to innumerable things.

5ᵇ34-6ᵃ4   44. A third sign, as well, is that if big were contrary to small, a single self-same thing would admit of two things contrary to each other at the same time. For a single self-same thing might be described as big and small, but in relation to two things. If it were so described in a contrary manner—I mean, essentially—and in the way body is described as being white and black, then the two contraries would exist in a single subject at the same time. Thus it would be possible for

---

[25] Literally, "in reference" (*bi al-qiyās*), "to something else" being added for clarity; usually, however, the term *ilā ghairih* (to something else) accompanies the term *bi al-qiyās*.

the thing to be white and black at the same time, and
that is absurd. Therefore it is not possible for two contraries to come together in a single subject at the same
time, not even in two different respects as is possible
with the rest of the opposites.

45. Moreover, if big were the contrary of small, the   6ᵃ5-10
thing would be contrary to itself, for a thing is described as being big and small at the same time. Now
if we postulate that these are contraries, it follows that
these two attributes would be attributes inhering in the
essence of a single self-same thing and the single self-
same thing would be big and small at the same time
so that it would necessarily be contrary to itself. And
that is extremely preposterous. So it has become clear
from this that neither big and small nor few and many
are contraries, whether we grant that they are quantity
or not.

46. He said: it is mainly with respect to the genus of   6ᵃ11-19
place that being contrary is presumed²⁶ to attach to
quantity, for the highest place, namely, the deepest
point of the celestial sphere, is presumed to be contrary
to the lowest place, namely, the middle of the world—
I mean, the place in the earth which is the deepest
point of water and of some air. Now they maintained
that these two places were contrary to each other because each is so extremely distant from the other that
nothing more distant could exist. And because of this
meaning becoming evident in these two, they extended
the definition to the rest of the contraries from this
name.²⁷ Thus in defining these two they said that they
are the ones which are most extremely distant and are
in one genus. However, they mean distance with respect to existence here, not distance with respect to
interval. I say: it seems that being contrary attaches to
quantity here insofar as it is place,²⁸ not insofar as it

²⁶ The verb translated here and later in the sentence as "presumed" (ẓann) is rendered as "supposed" in the rest of the treatise.
²⁷ That is, the name of place.
²⁸ Literally, "where" (ayn); see above, para. 17, note 2.

is quantity nor even insofar as it is relation—I mean, above and below. Instead, that is an accidental attribute of relation, just as it is an accidental attribute of quantity. Therefore one ought not to believe on the basis of this that contrariety attaches to relation.

CHAPTER SIX

6ª20-26   47. He said: one of the particular characteristics of quantity is that it does not admit of the lesser or the greater. For this designated quantity which is two cubits long is not greater than this other one which is also two cubits long. Nor is three greater than three. Moreover, it is not said of a particular time that it is more time than another time. However, quantity shares these two particular characteristics with substance—I mean, insofar as it has no contrary and insofar as it does not admit of the lesser or the greater.

CHAPTER SEVEN

6ª27-35   48. The thing which is most particularly character-istic of quantity is equality and inequality, for this is not attributed to anything other than quantity. For example, quality is not said to be equal or unequal, but is said to be similar or dissimilar. That is because we say that this whiteness is similar or dissimilar to this other whiteness and only accidentally say that it is equal or unequal to it. So for this reason what is most particularly characteristic of quantity is that it is equal or unequal.

SECTION THREE
ABOUT THE CATEGORY OF RELATION

49. What he speaks about with respect to this category consists of eight chapters.

The first is about a general description of relative things and an enumeration of them by means of examples.

The second is about there being contraries with respect to relatives.

The third is about some relatives admitting of the lesser and the greater.

The fourth is about one of the particular characteristics of relatives being that each one reciprocates with the other when they are designated by names which signify that they are relatives, if they have such a name or if such a name is invented for them when they do not have one.

The fifth is about relatives when they are designated by names which signify that they are relative and reciprocal. The attribute by which each is related to the other is distinguished from the rest of the attributes found in relatives in that when the rest of the attributes are eliminated and this one remains, the connection between the two relatives is not eliminated. And when this attribute is eliminated, so is the connection. If they are not designated as reciprocal, it does not result that when the rest of the things which are in the relatives are eliminated and this attribute by which each is connected with its mate remains, the connection remains.

The sixth is about one of the particular characteristics of relatives being that they exist simultaneously by nature and that when one is eliminated, so is the other. And the doubt which occurs with respect to that is resolved.

The seventh is about stating the doubt which may arise as to whether there is anything relative in substance. That doubt is resolved by considering the preceding general description of relation and modifying it by stipulating what truly pertains to relatives. For he had originally described it according to unexamined and generally accepted opinion, his intention being to make instruction easier. For it is easier to move the student from what is generally accepted to what is certain than to force certainty upon him from the outset. And it is said that this was Plato's general description.

The eighth is about the stipulation set down in the

general description of relatives to the effect that it be a general description particularly characteristic of them which makes their substances known, one of their particular characteristics thus being that when one of the two is known, the other is necessarily known and it therefore becoming clear that nothing enumerated as relative is in substance. In addition, he makes known that in spite of how easy it is for doubts to arise with respect to this topic, it is difficult to resolve those doubts. The reason is that his perspective here is that of what is generally accepted.

CHAPTER ONE

6ª37-6ᵇ14   50. He said: relative things are the ones whose quiddity and essence are spoken of in reference to something else, either essentially—like few and many—or by one of the particles of connection—like "to" and similar things. An example of this is that the quiddity of "bigger" is spoken of in reference to something else, for it is indeed bigger than something else. Likewise, "double" is double of something. State, condition, sense perception, and knowledge are relatives, for the quiddity of all of these is spoken of in reference to something else by means of one of the particles of connection. That is because state is a state of something; knowledge is of the knowable; and sense perception is of the perceptible. Likewise, big and small are spoken of in terms of relation. Likewise, the similar is similar to something. And to be lying down, to be standing up, and to be sitting belong to position, which is relation in some respect. Now "lies down," "stands up," and "sits" do not belong to position, but to things whose names are derived from position—that is, those in the category of position.

CHAPTER TWO

6ᵇ15-19   51. Relative things may happen to be contraries. For example, virtue and vice are relatives, and they are both contraries. Similarly, both knowledge and ignorance are relatives and contraries. However, this does not hold for all relative things. For there is no contrary of double, nor is there a contrary of triple.

CHAPTER THREE

52. Likewise, some relatives may admit of the lesser and the greater. For the similar and the dissimilar, the equal and the unequal, are all relatives, and one similar thing may be less or more so than another, just as may an unequal thing. Some do not admit this. For one double is not less nor more so than another, nor is one equal thing more so than another. 6^b20-27

CHAPTER FOUR

53. One of the particular characteristics of relatives is that each reciprocates with its correlative. For example, the slave is a slave of the master and the master is a master of the slave, the double is double of the half and the half is half of the double, and likewise with the rest. Regardless of whether the names of the relatives are different—as with the double and the half—or one is derived from the other—as with knowledge and the knowable or sense perception and the perceptible—each of these is spoken of in reference to the other. 6^b28-37

54. It may be supposed that this particular characteristic does not hold for many relative things when one of them is not related to the other in a balanced manner—that is, when neither one of them is related to the other by way of being a relation—but one is related to the other by way of being a relation and the other in an accidental manner or both are taken otherwise than by way of being a relation. For example, if wing were to be related to what is feathered and it were said "the wing is a wing of what is feathered," it would not be correct to state this as a reciprocation. For the connection between the wing and what is feathered is not by way of it being feathered, since something which has wings but no feathers may exist. So 6^b38-7^a18

the wing is not connected with it insofar as it is feathered, even though what is feathered is connected with the wing insofar as it is feathered. Therefore this is not a balanced relationship. When this is changed and a balanced connection is adopted so that it is said "what is winged is winged by dint of the wing," there is reciprocation—namely, "the wing is a wing of what is winged." Or we could say "what is feathered is what is winged with feathers" and "the wing with feathers is a wing of what is feathered." Therefore, when the balanced relationship does not have a name which signifies that it is balanced—and this either with respect to both correlatives or to one of them—the person making the relation will find it necessary to posit a name for both or for one of them inasmuch as he treats them as correlatives. For example, if rudder is related to boat, that is not a balanced relationship. For it is not insofar as the boat is a boat that rudder is related to it, since boats without rudders surely exist, yet rudder is indeed related to boat insofar as it is a rudder. Therefore there is no reciprocation so that it can be said "the boat is a boat of the rudder" the way it is said "the rudder is a rudder of the boat." However, in this instance if it were desired that both terms of the relationship be balanced and grasped in the same manner, one ought to say "the rudder is a rudder of the ruddered boat." Then it would be correct that the ruddered boat is a boat by dint of the rudder, for just as the rudder is only a rudder by dint of the boat, so, too, the boat which is such as to have a rudder is a boat by dint of the rudder. Another example is that when head is related to what is headed, the relationship is balanced; yet when it is related to the living being, the relationship is not balanced. For the living being does not have a head because it is a living being,[29] since animals without heads surely exist.

[29] Or, more literally, "by way of being alive" (*min ṭarīq mā huwa ḥayy*).

55. This is the way one ought to proceed in making   7ª18-30
relations about things which do not have a relative
name—I mean, to posit a name which signifies that the
relationship between the two related things is balanced,
as we said with respect to the wing and the rudder.
Now if this is the case, then whenever relatives are
taken in a balanced manner—that is, by way of being
relatives, not by way of falling under another category—they will always have this particular characteristic, namely, that each one of the correlatives reciprocates with the other. On the other hand, when they
are related to each other in a random manner and
according to any attribute whatever from among those
found in the correlatives and intrinsic to the relation,
not according to the attribute by which they are relatives and connected with one another, they will not
reciprocate. And this holds even if names with respect
to the way they are related have been posited for them,
not to mention those not having names which signify
the way they are related. For example, if "slave" is not
related to "master," which is the relative name, but to
"man," or to "being two-legged," or any of the similar
things existing in master, there is no reciprocation. For
a man is not a man by dint of having a slave, even
though he is surely a master by dint of having a slave.
So if master is substituted for man, there is reciprocation.

CHAPTER FIVE

56. A particular characteristic of this attribute by   7ª31-7ᵇ10
means of which the correlatives are connected is that
if we eliminate all the other accidental attributes of the
correlatives which make the relationship unbalanced,
the connection between the correlatives is not eliminated; yet if we eliminate this attribute, the connection
is eliminated. For example, if the slave is spoken of in
relation to the master and we eliminate from the master all the rest of the attributes to which the slave might

be connected—like his being a man, or being two-legged or other things—but do not eliminate his being a master, the connection between him and the slave is not eliminated. Yet when we relate the slave to man or to being two-legged and eliminate his having a master, this connection is eliminated, for there is no slave who does not have a master. Therefore the balanced connection is the one belonging to the attribute which is such that the connection is eliminated when it is eliminated, but is not eliminated when anything else is eliminated. What he mentioned here is like a rule for discerning which attribute has the balanced connection.

7ᵇ11-14   57. He said: it is easy to find this connection which makes the relationship balanced when the correlatives have a name which signifies that they have this connection but difficult when they do not have such a name. Then, however, that attribute ought to be inferred by means of this rule and a name invented for the correlatives which signifies that they have this connection.

CHAPTER SIX

7ᵇ15-8ᵃ12   58. He said: it may be supposed that one of the particular characteristics of correlatives is that they exist simultaneously by nature. With most of them, this is evident. The double and the half exist simultaneously, for when one exists so does the other, and when one is eliminated so is the other. However, a doubt may attach to that with respect to some relative things, for it may be supposed that the knowable is prior to knowledge since knowledge about something occurs in most instances only after it exists, and rarely at the very moment it exists. If this is so, then there is no single knowable thing which exists by nature simultaneously with the knowledge of it. Moreover, it is evident that the knowable is naturally prior to knowledge, because when the knowable is eliminated so is knowledge, but when knowledge is eliminated the knowable is not. And this, according to what will be said later, is the general description of what is prior by nature.[30] Take, for example, the squaring of the circle which earlier geometricians looked into without discovering: if it is knowable, knowledge of it does not yet exist; and if it is not knowable, then there can be no knowledge of it. Moreover, when man is eliminated, so is knowledge; yet the knowable may exist even though man does not. This self-same doubt attaches to sense perception and the perceptible. For it may be supposed that the perceptible is prior to sense perception, since with the loss of the perceptible comes the loss of sense perception whereas with the loss of sense perception there is no loss of the perceptible. Indeed, the loss of the perceptible results in the loss of sense perception insofar as the perceptible and sense perception only exist in body. For when the perceptible is eliminated, body is eliminated; and when body is eliminated, the sensing being and sense perception are eliminated. On the other hand, the perceptible is not eliminated due to sense perception being eliminated, for an animal may lose it and the perceptible body still exist—like the warm or the cold body. Moreover, sense perception and the living being exist simultaneously, whereas the perceptible has prior existence. For water, fire, and all the other elements which constitute animal exist before the animal does. Because of all this it may be supposed that the perceptible exists prior to sense perception.

59. The commentators resolve this doubt by maintaining that if sense perception and the perceptible or knowledge and the knowable are taken either potentially or actually, they exist simultaneously and that particular characteristic applies to them. For this doubt occurs only when one of the two is taken potentially and the other actually. However, since potential existence is not something which is generally accepted, he postponed the solution of this doubt for another oc-

[30] See below, para. 104.

casion. For he speaks about these things here only from the perspective of what is generally accepted. In truth, correlatives of this sort[31] do not exist simultaneously by nature, for as Aristotle says in the *Metaphysics* one of these correlatives is essential and the other is accidental.[32]

CHAPTER SEVEN

8ª13-28   60. He said: there is room for doubt as to whether anything relative can be in substance insofar as it is substance. This doubt occurs with respect to some secondary substances, but not with respect to primary substances. That is because it is evident that neither the whole nor a part of any of these can be spoken of as relative. For it is not said of this designated man that he is a man of a certain thing. The case is the same with designated parts. For it is not said of a designated hand that it is a certain man's hand or a certain horse's, but it is said to be a man's hand or a horse's. In general, the relation is made to the species, not to the individual. The case is evidently similar with respect to most secondary substances, for a man is not said to be a man of something, nor an ox said to be an ox of something insofar as it is an ox—I mean, a substance—but if this is done, then it is only with respect to its being someone's property. However, this doubt may hold for some of them. That is because it may be said that a head is a head of something, that a hand is a hand of something, and likewise with similar things. Now since hand and head do signify substance, it may be supposed that many substances fall under relation.

8ª29-36   61. He said: nonetheless if our saying that relatives are those things whose quiddities are spoken of in reference to something else constitutes an exhaustive def-

[31] Or, literally, "genus" (*jins*).
[32] See Aristotle *Metaphysics* V.xv.1021ª26-33 and also Averroes *Tafsīr Mā Baʿd al-Ṭabīʿah*, vol. II, pp. 617-618.

inition of relative things, then it will be difficult or impossible to resolve this doubt. That is because it has already become evident that these substances are such that their quiddities are spoken of in reference to something else.[33] Still, if the true general description of relative things is that they are two things such that the quiddity of each is spoken of in reference to the other as existing inasmuch as it is related to its mate in some kind of manner, then it is easy to resolve this doubt. For the first definition applies to everything which is considered as relative according to unexamined opinion, whereas this definition applies to what is in truth relative, not according to unexamined opinion.

62. As I see it, he meant by this that if head signifies substance, then it is related to man not by virtue of a true relation but by virtue of an accidental one—that is, one that does not pertain to the substance of the relative thing. This is the one included in the first general description, I mean, the accidental one. On the other hand, an example of the relationship which pertains to the substance of each correlative is the few and the many, for each of these pertains to the substance of its correlative. And this is the one included in the second general description, I mean, the true one.

CHAPTER EIGHT

63. He said: it is clear from this true definition of correlatives that one of their particular characteristics is that when a man definitely knows one of them, he necessarily knows the other. For when a man knows that this thing is a relative and that the quiddity of one of the correlatives exists inasmuch as it is connected to the second correlative, then it is clear that when he knows the quiddity of one of the correlatives he knows the quiddity of the other. Otherwise his knowledge of

8ª37-8ᵇ21

[33] See above, para. 50. The phrase "to something else" has been added here for clarity; see above, para. 42, note 25.

the quiddity of one of the correlatives is not knowledge of it as it really is, but supposition or error. That also becomes clear through induction. For example, someone who definitely knows that this is double definitely knows what it is double of. Likewise, someone who knows that this is better knows what it is better than, unless the knowledge is uncertain conjecture. For if he does not know the thing which is said to be better, it may be that there is nothing inferior to it in goodness, and his saying that it is better would be false. From this it appears that head and hand are not true relatives, for the quiddity of both, inasmuch as they are substance, may be definitely known without knowing what they are a head or hand of.

8ᵇ22-24   64. He said: in general, it is difficult to make a true judgment about which of the rest of the categories belong to relation and which do not without reflecting many times about them. However, having doubts about them presents no difficulty.[34]

SECTION FOUR
THE DISCUSSION OF QUALITY

65. What he says under this heading consists of eleven chapters.

In the first, he defines this category and explains that it is divided into primary genera.[35]

In the second, he makes known which of these genera has the name of state and condition. And he makes known which has the particular name of state—namely, the one which is said to be quality according to what

---

[34] Or "is not difficult" (*fa-lais fīh ṣa'ūbah*), either one of which seems to go against Aristotle's original (*ouk axrēston estin*) as well as against the Arabic translation (*fa-lais minmā lā dark fīh*). See above, para. 49.

[35] The term is, indeed, "genera" (*ajnās*). Throughout this section, Averroes uses the terms *jins* (genus) and *ajnās* (genera) as though he means "kind" (*naw'*) or "kinds" (*anwā'*). Yet if the categories are ultimate genera (see above, para. 13), it would be technically correct to speak of a given category consisting of subordinate genera; for this reason, I have preferred to translate these terms literally here.

is generally accepted—as well as which has the particular name of condition. He makes known that if these
are said to be quality, it is due to their being of one
nature.

In the third, he makes known the second genus in
this category—namely, the one which is said to be due
to a natural faculty or not due to a natural faculty.

In the fourth, he makes known the third genus in
this category—namely, affective qualities and affections. He makes known why they are called affective
qualities and distinguishes those which are called affective qualities from those which are called affections.
He makes known that, according to what is generally
accepted, the name quality applies only to affective
qualities for the same reason that it is applied to state
more than to condition.

In the fifth, he makes known the fourth genus in
this category—namely, quality found in quantity insofar as it is quantity.

In the sixth, he raises doubts about whether sparse,
dense, rough, and smooth fall under this category or
under the category of position.

In the seventh, he makes known that the things characterized as quality are those signified by names derived from the primary paradigms which signify this
category.

In the eighth, he makes known that contrariety may
be found in quality, but only in some of it. He also
makes known that if one of a pair of contraries is in
the category of quality, the other must inevitably be in
it.

In the ninth, he makes known that quality may admit
of the lesser and the greater, but not all of quality.

In the tenth, he makes known that the particular
characteristic of this category is the similar and the
dissimilar.

In the eleventh, he raises doubts about many things
mentioned under this heading, as well as under the

heading of relation. He shows what occasions this and
that it occurs in two ways.

CHAPTER ONE

8ᵇ25-26   66. He said: I call quality the characteristics which
are used to respond to the question about how individuals are. And these qualities are said of different
primary genera.

CHAPTER TWO

8ᵇ27-9ᵃ3   67. One is the genus of quality which is called state
and condition. State differs from condition in that it
is said of what in this genus is more durable and longer
lasting, whereas condition is said of what passes away
quickly. The sciences and the virtues are examples of
this. For when knowledge of something comes to be
an art, it is one of the firmly established things which
pass away with difficulty; that is, as long as no serious
change befalls a man due to sickness or something else,
like being preoccupied with the incidental affairs which
over time cause him to neglect his knowledge and to
forget it. On the other hand, condition is said of those
things in this genus which move quickly and change
easily—like health and sickness and heat and cold, which
are the causes of health and sickness. For the healthy
man soon becomes sick and the sick man healthy as
long as these conditions do not become fixed so that
they pass away with difficulty. For if that were the case,
man would have to call them states.

9ᵃ4-13   68. He said: it is clear that in Greek the name state
signifies things which are long established and moved
with difficulty. For they do not say of someone who
does not have a reliable grasp of knowledge that he is
in a state. However, someone of this description is in
a condition with respect to knowledge which is either
good or bad.³⁶ In one way, states are also conditions;

³⁶ Literally, "either noble or base" (*immā sharīfah wa immā khasīsah*).

but conditions are not states. Moreover, states are conditions at first, then they become states afterward. As has been said, this genus comprehends the characteristics found in the soul and in the animate being insofar as it is an animate being.

CHAPTER THREE

69. He said: there is a second genus of quality, and   9ª14-27
it is the one by which we say of something that it has a natural faculty or does not have a natural faculty—like our saying healthy or sickly. That is because something is not said to be healthy or sickly or whatever else because of its having a certain state in the soul or in the animate being insofar as it is animate, but because of its having a natural faculty or not having a natural faculty. By not having a natural faculty, I mean that it acts with difficulty and is affected easily; and by a natural faculty, I mean that it acts easily and is affected only with difficulty. For example, someone is said to be healthy because he has a faculty[37] such that he is not affected by sicknesses or epidemics. And we call someone a runner or a wrestler insofar as he has a faculty by which he does this easily and is affected with difficulty. And we say that someone is sickly because he does not have a natural faculty[37] such that he is not affected by sicknesses. It is the same with what is hard and soft, for something is said to be hard insofar as it has a faculty such that it is not easily affected and is said to be soft because it does not have a faculty such that it is not easily affected.

CHAPTER FOUR

70. He said: there is a third genus of quality, and it   9ª27-35
is the one which is spoken of as affective qualities and affections. The species of this are tastes—like the sweet and the bitter—and colors—like black and white—and

---

[37] Or "capacity" or "power." The Arabic term is *quwwah.*

tactile things—like heat, cold, moisture, and dryness. With all of these it is evident that they are such as to be qualities, for anything to which one of them is attributed may be asked about by using the particle "how." For example, we would say "how sweet is this honey" and "how white is this garment?" And the reply would be that it is very sweet and very white or not very sweet or white.

9ᵃ36-9ᵇ8   71. Now things like these are said to be affective qualities not because they occur in the things to which they are attributed by means of an affection, but because they give rise to an affection in our senses. For example, the sweetness in honey and the bitterness in aloes are said to be affective qualities not because of an affection giving rise to sweetness in honey nor because of an affection giving rise to bitterness in aloes, but because both of them give rise to an affection in the tongue. It is the same for heat and cold with the sense of touch.

9ᵇ9-33   72. What is in the third species—namely, colors—is not said to be affective qualities in this respect, since colors do not give rise to an affection in sight. Indeed, these are said to be affective qualities because they arise in the thing to which they are attributed due to an affection. That is because it is clear that the redness which accompanies embarrassment and the yellowness which accompanies fright arise from an affection which gets into the blood and the breath.[38] Consequently, we must necessarily believe that the cause of anyone being red or yellow originally and by nature is that in its early formation his make-up was affected by the kind of affection which brings about the redness accompanying embarrassment and the yellowness accompanying fright. Accidents like these which are firmly established and pass away with difficulty are called affective qualities and are usually asked about by means of the particle "how." Those which are quickly moved are not

---

[38] Or, perhaps, "animal spirit" (*al-rūḥ*).

called affective qualities, nor is it customary to ask about
them by means of the particle "how." Therefore, this
genus must be particularly characterized only by means
of the name "affection," not by means of the name
"affective quality." For example, when one of us is
yellow or red by nature and temperament, they are
used to speak of "how" that individual is. But when
the redness is occasioned by embarrassment or the yellowness by fright, they are not used to say "how" the
individual is. That is because someone in this condition
is not said to be reddened or yellowed, but is only said
to be red or yellow, and, in general, simply to be affected. So things like this must only be called affections,
even though they differ in length and shortness of
duration.

73. In the same manner, those accidents of the soul   9ᵇ34-10ᵃ10
which are natural and firmly established are said to be
affective qualities, whereas those which are accidental
and do not belong to man by nature or make-up are
said to be affections. Take for example insanity and
irascibility. Someone who naturally has these is said to
be irascible and insane. Thus, things like this are called
affective qualities. Yet someone who becomes angry
because of an embarrassing event befalling him is said
neither to be irascible nor insane, but only to have
become angry or to have lost his head. So things like
this must be said to be affections, not affective qualities.
That is because the form of this utterance is always
suited to that which is firmly established.

CHAPTER FIVE

74. He said: there is a fourth genus—namely, the   10ᵃ11-16
figure and shape found in each and every thing, as
well as straightness, crookedness, and the like. For
something is spoken of in terms of "how it is," when
one of these is attributed to it. This is because it is in
reply to "how is it," that something is said to be tri-

angular or square, straight or crooked. The same holds
with shape.

CHAPTER SIX

10ª17-25   75. It may be supposed that sparse and dense, as
well as rough and smooth, fall under this genus. Yet
one should rather believe that these two groups of
things[39] fall outside this genus. That is because it is
evident that each one more readily falls under the category of position than under this category. That is
because sparse and dense signify a certain position of
parts. For something whose parts are close to one another is said to be dense, while something whose parts
are distant from one another is said to be sparse. Likewise, something whose parts are equally placed along
its surface without any protruding over any others is
said to be smooth. And something whose parts are not
equally placed but has some protruding over others is
said to be rough.

10ª25-27   76. He said: perhaps some other qualities may become evident here, but this is the sum of the ones we
have enumerated here with respect to this genus.

77. He means that those other qualities are the qualities one asks about with respect to species by means
of the particle "how"—namely, things which are specific images or which follow from specific images. The
qualities discussed here are the qualities one asks about
with respect to individuals—namely, the conditions accompanying images because of matter and material
things. That is evident from the difference between
these two kinds of quality.

CHAPTER SEVEN

10ª28-10ᵇ12   78. He said: qualified things are those signified by
names[40] which signify the qualities themselves, that is,

[39] Literally, "these two genera" (*hādhaini al-jinsain*).
[40] Or "nouns" (*asmā*).

the primary paradigms. In the Greek language that comes about for most of them by means of derivation— like with "white" which is derived from the noun "whiteness," "eloquent" which is derived from the noun "eloquence," and "just" which is derived from the noun "justice." For some exceptional ones, that is, those qualities taken apart from the subject, there are no names in Greek; so names for those qualities are derived insofar as they are in a subject. For example, the names they set down for things falling under what is said to occur by means of a natural faculty or not by means of a natural faculty are not derived from anything— like runner and boxer. For the names which signify these notions for them are not derived from "running" nor from "boxing," as they are in the speech of the Arabs.[41] Nor is it unusual to find verbs in the Arabic language which have no verbal nouns. However, in the Greek language it sometimes happens that there will be a name for a quality insofar as it is apart from a subject, and insofar as it is in a subject the name of that quality will be derived from another name. For example, they used to say "diligent," not "virtuous," when referring to virtue.[42]

CHAPTER EIGHT

79. He said: contrariety may exist in quality. For   10b13-25
example, justice is the contrary of injustice, and white-

[41] Aristotle's point is that even though some people are runners or boxers because of a natural faculty and others because they have learned how to run or box, there is no name to distinguish the former from the latter; there are, however, nouns to denote running and boxing. Thus only insofar as someone learns the art of boxing can his being called a "boxer" be said to be derived from "boxing," but it does of course have all the formal characteristics of a derived noun.

[42] Aristotle's point is that the man who has virtue (aretē) is said to be spoudaios, there being no adjectival form of aretē. To catch the nuance, Averroes uses the term mujtahid, literally "one who strives"; to use this term in speaking of someone carries the connotation that his striving is for the glory of God.

ness is the contrary of blackness. It also exists in qualified things. For example, just is the contrary of unjust,
and white is the contrary of black. However, contrariety does not exist in all qualities nor in all qualified
things. For there is no contrary of blond, of yellow, or,
in general, of any of the intermediate qualities. Moreover, when one of two contraries falls under quality,
the other contrary falls under quality; and this becomes
evident by induction. For example, since just is contrary to unjust and falls under quality, unjust falls under quality. For it would not be correct for us to say
that unjust falls under quantity, relation, or any other
category. The same is evident with the rest of the contraries to be found in quality.

CHAPTER NINE

10ᵇ26-11ᵃ14   80. He said: quality may admit of the lesser and the
greater. For one man may be more just than another
or one thing whiter than another, since the subjects of
these things admit of the lesser and the greater. However, this is so only with some qualities, not with all.
Doubt about whether these qualities admit of the greater
and the lesser occurs when they are taken apart from
their subjects. One group of people contests this, setting forth the opinion that one justice is not more a
justice than another nor one health more a health than
another—even though one person may be more just
or healthier than another. The same holds with the
rest of this genus[43]—namely, condition. Now the triangle, the square, and the rest of the figures do not
admit of the greater and the lesser, for one triangle is
not more a triangle than another nor is one square
more a square than another. Anything falling under
the definition of triangle is equally a triangle. Likewise,
anything falling under and accepting the definition of
square is equally set down as a square. Whatever does
not fall under the definition of something is not spoken

[43] See above, para. 65, note 35.

of in reference to it, for no one says that the square is more circular than the oblong. In general, then, references are correct only with respect to things falling under a single definition. Now if this is so, not every quality admits of the greater and the lesser, nor is any of the things we have mentioned a true particular characteristic of quality.

CHAPTER TEN

81. The true particular characteristic of quality, which applies to nothing else, is the similar and the dissimilar.   11ᵃ15

CHAPTER ELEVEN

82. He said: no one ought to suspect this argument and say that even though the intention here was to enumerate qualities, many things belonging to relation have been enumerated—like state and condition, which were enumerated in the first genus of this category and which fall under relation. For state is a state of something, and the same with condition. Now these can be enumerated as relation in terms of their genera, but not in terms of their species. Knowledge—which is the genus of grammar and jurisprudence—can be spoken of in relation to the knowable. But neither grammar nor jurisprudence can be spoken of in relation to anything, unless they be spoken of in terms of their genus—I mean, as grammar being knowledge of the knowable, that is, knowledge of the endings of words. Since these species are not relation but quality and they have become species of quality only because of their genus, it is clear that their genus is quality. That is, grammar and jurisprudence each come to be only inasmuch as knowledge is quality. However, their genus—namely, knowledge—happens to have a name inasmuch as it is relation but none inasmuch as it is quality, contrary to what happens to the species which are under it—I mean, that they have names inasmuch as they are qualities, like grammar and jurisprudence,   11ᵃ20-38

but none inasmuch as they are relations. It is not unusual for a single thing to be counted in two categories
and two genera, as long as that is in two respects and
not a single respect. For that would be absurd.

83. This is the way in which Abū Naṣr [al-Fārābī]
interpreted this subject.[44] The evident sense of Aristotle's language is that these belong to relation only by
dint of their genus, since grammar and music are to
be understood as having a relation particularly characteristic of them only because of their genus. Therefore what Aristotle says about these things not being
relations essentially and their having come to be relations only because of what is a relation essentially
being related to them means that they are relations
accidentally. It is not unusual for a single thing to fall
under two genera, under one essentially and under
the other accidentally. However, it would be unusual,
just as Aristotle says, for a single thing to exist essentially in two different genera.

SECTION FIVE

THE DISCUSSION OF DOING AND BEING ACTED UPON

11ᵇ1-8   84. He said: doing and being acted upon may admit
of contrariety and of the greater and the lesser. For
heating is contrary to cooling, being cooled contrary
to being heated, and being delighted contrary to being
pained. So this genus admits of contrariety as well as
of the lesser and the greater. Our saying that something is "being heated" may be greater or less, for it
may be heated more or less. Likewise, one may be
pained to a greater or lesser degree.[45]

11ᵇ8   85. He said: this is the sum of what we will say about
this category in this context.

[44] See "Al-Fārābī's Paraphrase of the 'Categories' of Aristotle," ed.
D. M. Dunlop, *The Islamic Quarterly*, IV (1957), pp. 168-183, and V
(1959), pp. 21-37, paras. 27-28.

[45] Literally, "be more or less pained" (*yata'adhā akthar wa aqall*).

SECTION SIX
ABOUT THE CATEGORY OF POSITION

86. He said: the things which are in a position were   11ᵇ8-10
mentioned under the heading of relation. It was said
that they are the things whose names are derived from
the category of relation—like lying down and reclining.[46] Now to be lying down and to be reclining belong
to the category of relation, whereas lying down and
reclining belong to this category.

87. He said: with respect to the rest of the categories   11ᵇ10-15
which we have enumerated—namely, the category when,
the category where, and the category to have—nothing
in addition to the examples we gave of them at the
beginning of this book will be said about them here,
for they were quite clear. For instance, our saying that
"to have" signifies being shod and being armed, that
"where" is like our saying so-and-so is in the market,
and the other examples we set forth about them.[47] Now
this discussion of these genera is sufficient for our pur-
poses here.

[46] See above, para. 50.
[47] See above, para. 15.

PART THREE

This Part Is Divided into Five Sections

SECTION ONE
THE DISCUSSION OF OPPOSITES

88. What he speaks about under this heading consists of eleven chapters.

In the first, he enumerates the sorts of opposites and makes each and every one known by means of an example.

In the second, he differentiates opposites which are relatives from those which are contraries.

In the third, he makes it known that there are two kinds of contrary things.

In the fourth, he makes known the nature of things which are opposed with respect to privation and state.[1] And he makes it known that the things which have privation and state are neither privation itself nor state itself, even though they are opposed in the same way as privation and state are opposed.

In the fifth, he makes it known that things affirmed and negated are not the same as affirmative and negative propositions, even though they are opposed in the same way as affirmative and negative propositions[2] are opposed.

In the sixth, he makes known the difference between state and privation on the one hand and relatives on the other.

In the seventh, he makes known the difference be-

---

[1] See above, paras. 67, 68, and 82. In this discussion, the term rendered as "state" (*malakah*) could also be understood as "possession."

[2] The word "propositions" has been added for clarity.

tween privation and state on the one hand and contraries on the other.

In the eighth, he makes known the difference between affirmative and negative propositions[2] on the one hand and the three remaining opposites on the other—I mean, privation and state, relatives, and contraries. In doing so he resolves a doubt which occurs with respect to the way he differentiated contraries.

In the ninth, he makes it known that one single thing may be contrary to another single thing and that it may be contrary to two things.

In the tenth, he makes it known that the existence of one of two contraries does not result in the existence of the other. This is the particular characteristic which exists with respect to relatives.[3]

In the eleventh, he makes it known that every pair of contraries either falls under a single genus, under two contrary genera, or themselves constitute two contrary genera which do not fall under a single genus.

CHAPTER ONE

89. He said: there are four sorts of opposites—relatives, contraries, privation and state, and affirmative and negative propositions.[4] An example of relation is double and half. An example of contraries is good and evil. An example of privation and state is blindness and sight. An example of affirmative and negative propositions[4] is your saying "Zayd is sitting," "Zayd is not sitting."   11ᵇ16-24

CHAPTER TWO

90. The difference between relatives and contraries is that the quiddity of one of the correlatives, whichever one is chanced upon, is spoken of in reference to the other either as it is in itself or by means of any chance   11ᵇ25-38

---

[3] See above, para. 58.
[4] The word "propositions" has been added for clarity.

particle of connection—like the double which is spoken of in reference to the half. With contraries, the quiddity of one is not spoken of in reference to the other; rather, the quiddity of one is spoken of as the contrary of the quiddity of the other. Thus good is not said to be the good of evil, but the contrary of it; nor is white said to be the white of black, but the contrary of it. These two sorts of opposites are necessarily different.

CHAPTER THREE

11ᵇ38-12ᵃ25   91. Contraries which are such that the subject characterized by them is never free of one or the other are contraries having no intermediate between them—like health and sickness, the animate body never being free of one of them; or like even and odd, number never being free of one of them. There are no intermediates between contraries like these. Now contraries which are such that one of them is not necessarily found in their subject are contraries which do have an intermediate between them—for example, the blackness and whiteness which exist in body. Since it is not necessary that every colored body be either white or black and body may even be free of both of them, there must be intermediates between them—namely, yellow, gray, and the rest of the colors which are between white and black. It is the same with the praiseworthy and the blameworthy. Since it is not necessary that every thing be either praiseworthy or blameworthy, intermediates exist between them as well—namely, what is neither praiseworthy nor blameworthy. The intermediates with respect to some matters have names—like gray and yellow. Others have no names and are expressed by negating the two extremes—like our saying "neither good[5] nor bad" and "neither just nor unjust."

[5] Here the term is *jayyid* rather than *khair*, which also means "good" and which alone has been used heretofore.

CHAPTER FOUR

92. Now privation and state exist in a single self-   12ᵃ26-35
same thing. For example, sight and blindness exist in
the eye. In general, with this genus of privation, the
subject loses the state which it is its wont to have and
does so at the moment in which it is its wont to have
it, without it being possible for it to have that state in
the future. Thus only those who have no teeth at the
moment in which it is their wont to have them are said
to be toothless. And only those who have no sight at
the moment in which it is their wont to have sight are
said to be blind. Thus, the offspring of animals which
are born without teeth or sight—like puppies—are not
said to be toothless or blind.

93. He said: the thing which is deprived of state and   12ᵃ36-12ᵇ5
which has state is not privation and state. For example,
even though sight is a state and blindness its privation,
the one having sight is not sight and the one having
blindness is not blindness. If the underlying subject of
sight and sight were a single thing and the underlying
subject of blindness and blindness a single thing, it
would be correct to predicate sight of the seeing person
and blindness of the blind person and then to say "the
blind person is blindness" and "the one who sees is
sight." However, just as privation and state are opposites, so, too, are the things characterized by them
opposites. So if blindness is opposed to sight, the blind
person is opposed to the seeing person. That is because
they are opposites in the same respect.

CHAPTER FIVE

94. He said: likewise, that which is negated or af-   12ᵇ6-16
firmed is not the affirmative or negative proposition,[6]
for the affirmative proposition is an affirmative state-

---

[6] Throughout this paragraph, the term "proposition" has been
added for clarity. Though Averroes uses only the terms *al-mūjibah*
(the affirmative) and *al-sālibah* (the negative), both the context and
the earlier explanation of the contents of this chapter (see above,
para. 88) seem to demand such an addition.

ment and the negative proposition is a negative statement. What is affirmed or negated is not a statement,
but an idea signified by an uncombined utterance or
what has the same force as an uncombined utterance.
That which is affirmed or negated is opposed in the
same way as the affirmative proposition and the negative proposition are opposed. For example, just as our
saying "Zayd is sitting" is opposed to our saying "Zayd
is not sitting," so, too, sitting is opposed to not sitting.

CHAPTER SIX

12ᵇ17-25   95. It becomes evident that privation and state are
not opposed in the way relatives are from the fact that
with things opposed in the manner state and privation
are, the quiddity of one is not spoken of in reference
to the other, whereas that does happen with the quiddity of things opposed in the manner relatives are. For
it is not said that sight is the sight of blindness nor that
blindness is the blindness of sight so as to say "blindness
of sight."⁷ There is another difference as well, namely,
that each correlative reciprocates with the other, as has
been said.⁸ Yet things which are opposed in the manner of privation and state do not reciprocate with each
other. That is because sight is not sight of blindness
nor is blindness blindness of sight, which is state.

CHAPTER SEVEN

12ᵇ26-13ᵃ17   96. It also becomes evident from the following considerations that privation and state are not opposed in

⁷ In the passage which corresponds to this, Aristotle explains that
"privation of sight" (*sterēsis opseōs*) could be said. Even though the
phrase was rendered accurately in the Arabic translation as *ʿadam
li al-baṣr*, all of the manuscripts of Averroes' commentary have *ʿamā
al-baṣr* (blindness of sight). Since Averroes follows Aristotle in taking
blindness as an example of privation and sight as an example of
state, he apparently considers it as inappropriate to speak of the
privation of sight as to speak of the privation of a state, that is,
blindness of sight.

⁸ See above, paras. 53-55.

the same manner as contraries. That is, opposition involving contraries is concerned either with those contraries which have no intermediate between them or
with those which do have intermediates between them.
As has been said, the former sort is particularly characterized by the fact that the subject ascribed to them
is never free of one or the other of them—like health
and sickness, the body of the animal never being free
of one of them.[9] The latter sort is particularly characterized by the fact that its subject may be free of both
contraries as long as neither of them exists for it by
nature—like the heat existing in fire or the cold existing in ice, for fire is not free of heat nor ice of cold.[10]
If that is so, then contraries which have an intermediate
between them are never free of one of two features:
either one of the contraries definitely exists in the subject and never quits it, or the subject is free of both
contraries. Now none of these particular characteristics
which are found in the different sorts of contraries is
found in privation and state. That is because with opposition involving privation and state, it is not always
necessary that one of the two exist in that which receives them. However, that is necessary at the moment
in which that which receives them is wont to receive
one of the two. For example, that which is wont to see
may be without either sight or blindness[11]—like the
puppy, for it is not said to be blind nor to have sight.
Now the subject of contraries which have no intermediate between them is at no time whatever without
one of the two. Therefore privation and state are neither contraries which have no intermediate between
them nor are they contraries which have an intermediate between them. That is because with opposition

[9] See above, para. 91.

[10] This is the end of a long statement in the Arabic which begins
with the words "that is, opposition involving" and which fully explains the first sort of contraries before discussing the second.

[11] The words "sight or blindness" have been added for clarity; the
text has simply "may be without either one" (*qad yakhlū min kilaihimā*).

involving state and privation, one of the two opposites must exist in the subject at the moment in which it is its wont to have a state. This does not hold with respect to the sort of intermediates which does not always have one of the two contraries existing in the subject, for the subject may be without either of them. Nor can privation and state be said to be contraries which have an intermediate between them, one of which always exists in the subject. For there is no privation and state such that one of the two always exists in the subject. If that is so, then it has become clear that opposition with respect to privation and state is none of the sorts of opposition with respect to contrariety.

13ᵃ18-37   97. The sort of privation we described above may be further differentiated from opposition with respect to contrariety: either of the two contraries can change into the other as long as one of the two does not naturally and perpetually exist in the subject—like the heat in fire.[12] That is because the white may become black, the black may become white, the righteous man may become villainous, and the villainous man may become righteous. As Aristotle says, the latter occurs when he is brought into association with people who have virtuous doctrines and noble conduct. For association with virtuous people may bring a man into the path of virtue, even if only slightly. When he begins to move toward virtue, the movement becomes easier as time goes on. Thus he will either attain a considerable measure of virtue or completely attain it, if time does not prevent it. Now with this sort of privation and state, it is state which changes into privation. It is not possible for privation to change into state, since in defining it we said "without it being possible for it to have that state in the future."[13] Thus, it is not possible for the blind man to gain sight again nor for the bald man to have a luxuriant head of hair.

[12] See above, paras. 92, 93, and 95.
[13] See above, para. 92.

CHAPTER EIGHT

98. He said: it is clear that the opposition with respect to negation and affirmation is none of these three sorts of opposition. It is particularly characteristic of affirmative and negative propositions[14] as distinguished from these other things, that one of the two is necessarily true and the other false. This does not result with any   13ᵇ1-11
of the others. For example, with the contraries of health and sickness, it is not said that one of the two is true or false. The case is the same with opposition involving relatives—like the double and the half—and those involving state and privation—like blindness and sight. In general, when these three are designated by uncombined utterances or by what has the force of uncombined utterances, they are characterized by neither truth nor falsehood. Thus our saying "animal" is neither true nor false until we combine it with something else and say "man is an animal," and "is not an animal."

99. It may be supposed that when opposites with respect to contrariety on the one hand and privation and state on the other are said of other things, they have something in common with affirmative and negative propositions.[15] I mean, when they are denoted by a combined utterance which reports something—   13ᵇ12-35
like our saying by means of contraries, "Socrates is sick," "Socrates is healthy," both statements being contraries; or like our saying "Zayd is blind," "Zayd has sight." However, the difference between these two statements on the one hand and affirmative and negative propositions[15] on the other is that with things opposed as contraries in this respect, one of the two is always true or false only when the subject characterized by it exists. For example, with our saying "Socrates is sick," "Socrates is healthy," one of these two statements

---

[14] Literally, "the affirmative and the negative"; the word "propositions" has been added for clarity.
[15] See preceding note.

is true and the other false only when Socrates exists. When he does not exist, both statements are false. For things opposed with respect to privation and state—like our saying "Zayd is blind," "Zayd has sight"—one of the two is always true and the other false only under two conditions. One is that Zayd exist and the other that he exist at the moment in which it is his wont to have sight. For if Zayd does not exist, it is false to say that he is blind or that he has sight. Likewise, both are false at the moment in which he is in the womb. However, with affirmative and negative propositions,[15] one of the two is always true and the other always false whether the subject exists or not. Thus, when we say "Socrates is sick," "Socrates is not sick," one of the two is necessarily true and the other false whether Socrates exists or not. By means of this particular characteristic, opposition involving affirmation and negation is distinguished from the rest of the compound propositions belonging to the other opposites.

CHAPTER NINE

13ᵇ36-14ᵃ6   100. He said: evil is necessarily the contrary of good. That is clear from the inductive enumeration of particular evil and good things. For health is contrary to sickness, injustice is contrary to justice, cowardice is contrary to courage, and so on with other things. Now the contrary of evil is sometimes two things, one being good and the other evil. For cowardice—which is evil—is contrary to rashness—which is evil—and courage—which is good—is contrary to both. This is the case with goods which are intermediary between extremes which are evil. However, something like this occurs only rarely in this genus. Most often, good is the contrary of evil.

CHAPTER TEN

14ᵃ7-13   101. He said: with contraries it results that the existence of one contrary does not necessarily lead to the existence of the other. That is, if all animals are healthy, then sickness does not exist. And if all things are white, then blackness does not exist. Moreover, when Socrates is sick, it does not result that Plato is healthy. Yet it is not possible for Socrates to be healthy and sick simultaneously.

102. He said: every pair of contraries is such as to be in a single subject—like the health and sickness existing in the body of the living being, the whiteness and blackness existing in body simply, and the justice and injustice existing in the soul of man.

CHAPTER ELEVEN   14ª14-18

103. Every pair of contraries either falls under a single self-same genus—like white and black, whose proximate genus is color—or under two contrary genera—like justice and injustice, for the genus of justice is virtue and the genus of injustice is vice, and they are contraries—or they themselves constitute two contrary genera which have no higher genus—like good and   14ª19-25
evil. He means, when one is in one category and the other in another category; for when they are in one category, that category is their genus.

SECTION TWO
THE DISCUSSION OF PRIOR AND POSTERIOR

104. He said: one thing is said to be prior to another   14ª26-14ᵇ9
in four ways. The first and most well known is being prior in time, in the way we say that this is further advanced in years than another or more mature than another. The second is being prior by nature, namely, the one which exists when what is posterior exists and whose elimination entails the elimination of what is posterior. Yet this has no reciprocation in existence— I mean, that when the prior exists, the posterior exists. Rather, the elimination of the prior entails the elimi-

nation of the posterior, without the elimination of the posterior entailing the elimination of the prior—like the priority of one over two. For when two exists, one exists; yet when one exists, two does not necessarily exist. Now it is known that whatever exists because something else exists, without that other thing existing because it exists, is said to be prior to it. The third is being prior in rank, as is said with respect to the sciences and the arts. For the definitions and the general descriptions which the geometricians set down for the figures are prior in rank of knowledge to what they wish to demonstrate. With writing, knowledge of the letters of the alphabet is prior to learning writing. Likewise, the introductory statements in rhetorical speeches are prior to the goal intended by the rhetorical speech. The fourth is being prior in nobility and perfection, for what is more noble by nature is believed to be prior to what is less noble. Therefore you find this belief to be common to all people, even though this type of priority is quite distant from the preceding ones. That is because this sort of priority is more noble than the other ones.

14ᵇ10-23   105. He said: these four ways are just about the sum of the ways of speaking about priority according to unexamined opinion. However, there is another type of priority here, namely, priority as being the cause of something. It is the one which reciprocates with respect to existence resulting. I mean, when the prior thing which is the cause of the posterior thing exists, the posterior thing exists; and when the posterior thing exists, the prior thing exists. For example, a man's existence is prior to the correct belief that he exists. When a man exists, this belief about him exists; and when this belief exists, a man exists. The man is the cause of this belief existing, not the belief the cause of the man existing. That is because the cause of truth and falsehood in speech is the external existence of the thing characterized by one of the two opposites.

Now if this is another type of priority, then priority is spoken of in five ways.

SECTION THREE
THE DISCUSSION OF THE MEANING OF SIMULTANEOUS

106. Simultaneous is spoken of in two ways. The 14^b24-15^a8 better known way and the one said in an absolute sense is when two things come to be at the same time. For when one of the two is not prior to the other in time, they are said to be simultaneous in time. The second is when they are said to be simultaneous by nature, and there are two classes of this. One is for two things to reciprocate with respect to existence resulting. That is, when one of the two exists, the other exists, without one being the cause of the other's existence—like double and half, for when double exists, half exists; and when half exists, double exists; yet one is not the cause of the other. The second class is the co-ordinate species of the genus. I mean, those by which a genus is divided into primary divisions—like flying, swimming, and walking. These are the co-ordinate species of animal, which is their genus, and none of these is prior or posterior to another. Consequently, things like these are said to be simultaneous by nature. Each one of these co-ordinate species may be further divided into other species, and these will also be simultaneous by nature—like when we divide walking into what has two legs, four legs, many legs, and no legs. Now the genera of these species are prior to them by nature. That is because they do not reciprocate with them in existence. Thus when the swimming being exists, the living being exists; yet when the living being exists, it does not result that the swimming being exists.

107. As we have said, there are two sorts of things 15^a8-12 that are said to be simultaneous by nature. One is when one of two things reciprocates with the other with respect to existence resulting, yet is not the cause of the

other. The second are species which are co-ordinate, that is, each one of which is co-ordinate with the other. Those which are said to be simultaneous in an absolute sense are those which come into being at a single time.

SECTION FOUR
THE DISCUSSION OF MOTION

15ᵃ13-33   108. There are six kinds of motion: coming to be; its opposite, passing away; increase; its opposite, diminution; alteration; and change of place, which in our language is called *nuqlah*.[16] It is evident that all of these six kinds of motion except alteration are different from one another. For no one would suppose that coming to be is passing away, that increase is diminution, or that change of place[17] is any of these. Yet alteration may be supposed to be the same as the rest of the motions which we have enumerated. Alteration exists in all four of the genera of quality which we enumerated or in most of them, but none of the other motions has anything in common with it nor results from it. What moves in any one of the qualities does not necessarily increase or diminish, and likewise with the rest of the motions. Thus the motion of alteration must not be like any one of the other motions. If it were the same as one of the other motions or if one of them resulted from it, what is altered would necessarily increase, diminish, or be changed by one of the other sorts of change. This is not the way things are. The opposite of this would also result, namely, that what increases or moves in some other way would also be altered. But such is not the case. If the thing which gives rise to the surface called gnomon is added to the square in the art of geometry, it is increased; yet it does

---

[16] That is, "transfer."

[17] Literally, "transfer" (*nuqlah*), but Averroes has just indicated that this is the proper Arabic term to denote "change of place," otherwise rendered as *al-taghayyur fī al-makān*.

not undergo alteration. The same holds with all other things of this sort. From that it necessarily follows that these motions which we have enumerated here are different from one another.

109. The proof which he employed here is a persuasive one.[18] For the name increase is applied to this meaning only in a figurative manner. In truth, whatever increases undergoes alteration. The same holds with whatever comes into being. It is only what moves with respect to place that does not result in alteration. However, in a context like this, none of this is clear. Thus, since his intention was only to make it clear that alteration is different from the rest of the motions, he resorted to persuasion here.

110. He said: the contrary of absolute motion—which 15b1-16 is the genus—is absolute rest—which is likewise the genus of things at rest. The contrary of particular motions are particular instances of rest and particular motions. For example, rest in place is the contrary of change in place, passing away is the contrary of coming to be, and diminution is the contrary of increase. Likewise, it seems that motion with respect to place is the contrary of motion with respect to place when the position toward which there is motion is contrary. For example, motion upward is the contrary of motion downward, since up is the contrary of down. Now it is not easy to find a contrary, either with respect to rest or with respect to motion, for the remaining kind of motion which we enumerated—namely, alteration. It would seem as though it is to be believed that alteration has no contrary, unless someone were to propose that the rest opposed to it is rest in quality and that the motion opposed to it is motion in the quality which is contrary to the quality wherein that motion takes place, just as if he were to propose that the opposite of motion with respect to place is rest with respect to place or

---

[18] That is, *only* a persuasive proof. See above, para. 59.

motion[19] to the place contrary to which the other motion tended. For example, the contrary of change to blackness would be change to whiteness as well as rest in whiteness.

SECTION FIVE
THE DISCUSSION OF TO HAVE

15ᵇ17-29   111. To have is spoken of in diverse ways. One is with respect to state and condition, for we say that we have knowledge and that we have virtue. The second is with respect to quantity, for it is said that something has length of such and such an extent. The third is with respect to what covers the body, either all of it—like a garment or a robe—or part of it—like a ring on the finger and a sandal on the foot. According to the commentators, this third meaning is the one which is particularly characteristic of the category of to have. The fourth concerns the connection between the part and the whole—like our saying "he has a hand," and "he has a leg." The fifth is one which it was customary for the Greeks to employ. It concerns the connection between a thing and its receptacle—like wheat with respect to the measure of grain and wine with respect to the jug. For they had the custom of saying "the jug has wine," and "the grain measure has wheat." The sixth is with respect to possession—like our saying "he has money," "he has a wife," and "he has a house."

15ᵇ29-31   112. He said: however, this last meaning of to have is the most farfetched of these ways of speaking about to have, for our saying "he has a wife" signifies nothing more than being united.

15ᵇ31-33   113. He said: perhaps a meaning of to have other

---

[19] Or, more literally, "moving" (*al-taḥarruk*). Note, however, that the discussion here and in the preceding two paragraphs has centered on "motion" (*al-ḥarakah*).

than the ones we have enumerated will become evident from our discussion. Nonetheless, the generally accepted meanings of it are these we have enumerated, and in this respect they are sufficient.

The Middle Commentary on the *Categories* is ended.

AVERROES'
MIDDLE COMMENTARY
ON ARISTOTLE'S
DE INTERPRETATIONE

INTRODUCTION

I

When Averroes' *Middle Commentary on Aristotle's De Inter-pretatione* is compared with his *Middle Commentary on Aristotle's Categories*, a number of striking differences come to light. First, whereas he begins his discussion of Aristotle's *Categories* by explaining that he intends to comment upon that work as he has done on other works by Aristotle, he says nothing of the sort here. Secondly, although he carefully explains the structure of Aristotle's *Categories* and how the work is divided, as well as what Aristotle sought to accomplish in each part, he says nothing about the structure of the *De Interpretatione*. He simply divides his commentary into five chapters, each chapter corresponding to one or more chapters of Aristotle's text as we now know it, and embarks upon an explanation of the subject to which Aristotle addressed himself. Even the famous *qāl* (he said), the verb signifying that what follows is a quotation from Aristotle, is all but absent from this treatise. Although it occurs very frequently in the *Middle Commentary on Aristotle's Categories*, it occurs only five times here. And Averroes uses this sign in a very unusual way in his commentary. The first word of the treatise is *qāl*, but it is followed by an extremely free quotation from Aristotle. Then, in two of the four other uses of the verb, it is followed by statements having no parallel whatsoever in Aristotle's text.[1]

This treatise differs from the *Middle Commentary on Aristotle's Categories* and from other middle commentaries by Averroes in additional ways. References to Aristotle are

---

[1] See below, *Middle Commentary on Aristotle's De Interpretatione*, paras. 85 and 93, also paras. 82 and 83, which have no parallel in Aristotle's text. In para. 13, Averroes uses this quotation formula indirectly by speaking of "what he said" (*mā qālah*).

very rare: Averroes mentions Aristotle's name directly only three times in the whole commentary and refers to him obliquely only three additional times.[2] Conversely, he speaks frequently in his own name, either announcing what he is about to say (*naqūl*) or reminding the reader of things he has said or described. And on at least three occasions, he draws the reader's attention to something he is about to say by speaking in the first person singular (*aqūl*).[3] Finally, Averroes treats Aristotle's text quite cavalierly throughout this commentary. Although he follows the general order of Aristotle's exposition, he strays excessively from its content. Frequently, a point made by Aristotle is transformed in the course of the discussion into something quite different. Likewise, in passages amounting to almost one fifth of the commentary, Averroes launches into discussions that find no parallel in Aristotle's original text.[4]

Now these anomalies are not cited in order to suggest that this is anything other than a middle commentary or to cast doubt on its attribution to Averroes. They are mentioned only to give a rapid overall impression of the treatise and to underline the contention that it is impossible to provide a rigid superficial framework to which Averroes' middle commentaries must adhere. There is, after all, a very sound reason for Averroes to have taken such remarkable liberties with Aristotle's text. The problem which lies at the core of the treatise, the relationship between nature and convention with respect to language and meaning, prompts such action. Both Aristotle and Averroes begin their treatises by noting that the utterances men use to express their thoughts, just as the written symbols they use to designate those utterances, differ from nation to nation. Differently stated, both begin their treatises with the rec-

---

[2] See below, paras. 8, 15, and 47 as well as paras. 2, 16, and 84.

[3] He uses the first person singular in paras. 69, 75, and 76 and the more conventional first person plural in paras. 1, 2, 3, 24, 27, 28, 35, 47, 52, 60, 61, 62, 64, 65, 82, 85, 86, 87, 88, and 93. In paras. 1, 60, 62, 64, 82, and 86, this formula occurs twice.

[4] See below, paras. 27, 39, 42, 43, 44-46, 49, 52, 60, 64, 77, 78, 81, and 87; also paras. 40-41.

ognition that language is basically conventional. Although that statement must be modified, it means at the outset that Averroes discerns the need to adapt what Aristotle said in Greek about language and meaning to what is appropriate for Arabic. Nothing in Aristotle's *Categories* called for such an adaptation, for the subject of that work was the perception of attributes as they occur to all men. This substantive difference between the two works may be signalled by yet another superficial feature of the text before us, Averroes' numerous references to the Arabic language and to its limits or possibilities.[5]

II

As has been noted, Averroes divides his commentary into five chapters. The first, which serves as an introduction to the rest of the work, is further divided into three discussions—a discussion about the noun, a discussion about the verb, and one about the sentence. The first two discussions prepare the way for the discussion of the subject which both Aristotle and Averroes take to be the goal of the book: the declarative sentence (*al-qawl al-jāzim*).[6] Here, the task is to provide a general account of the parts of the sentence, especially the noun and the verb, and to distinguish the declarative sentence from non-declarative as well as from incomplete sentences. Although Aristotle's account of these subjects is dispersed over six chapters in the version of his text that has come down to us, he clearly indicated that his explanation of them was meant to serve as an introduction to the work by stating at the very beginning that these were the things he first wanted to talk about.[7]

The discussion in this introductory section is basically one of terminology for Aristotle as well as for Averroes. Each opens his treatise by identifying the utterance (*phōnē, lafz*) as the genus of which the noun and verb are species. Then each moves to a detailed explanation of the basic

---

[5] See below, paras. 9, 10, 11, and 19; also paras. 24, 40, and 50.

[6] See below, para. 16 with Aristotle *De Interpretatione* 17ª8.

[7] See Aristotle *De Interpretatione* 16ª1-3.

characteristics of the noun, the verb, and the sentence. Yet in tandem with this technical discussion of basic terminology, two other discussions are conducted—one centering on the problem of the relationship of language to convention and nature, the other concerning the place of truth and falsehood in language. Averroes appears to be especially desirous of explaining the conventional character of language. Aristotle's opening observation on the way spoken utterances resemble written letters prompts Averroes to identify the reason for that resemblance: utterances and written letters owe their origin to convention rather than to nature. Then, Aristotle's subsequent observation concerning the unvarying character of the ideas in the soul calls forth a longer explanation from Averroes. He contends that these ideas are the same for all human beings and that they are something like images in the soul of the beings which exist by nature.[8] However, these ideas or images do not themselves exist in the human soul by nature. We acquire them primarily by learning and study, but we do have standards by which to judge these acquisitions—namely, our understanding of the natural world, an understanding that is accessible to all normally intelligent human beings.

At this point Averroes follows Aristotle's lead and interrupts the discussion, sending the reader to the *De Anima* for a further account. Apparently, neither Aristotle nor Averroes wishes to introduce here that larger question of how our ideas or concepts reflect the world around us. Each seems to be more interested in pursuing the limited question of how language works and thus willing to leave aside for now the larger question of how it corresponds to reality. That larger question can either be answered in historical terms—that is, explaining how men actually formed language and how it evolved—or it can be answered in psychological terms—that is, by identifying that aspect of the human soul which permits man to name things and explaining how it functions. By referring us to the *De Anima*,

[8] See below, para. 2 with Aristotle *De Interpretatione* 16ª4-9.

our authors indicate their preference for the latter approach.

Nonetheless, that reference to the further discussion of meaning and nature in the *De Anima* does not signify that the subject of the conventional character of language is closed. It returns when our authors begin to explain what a noun is. Each emphasizes that a noun is an utterance which has meaning due to convention alone. And each insists on the conventional origin of meaning, because each denies that utterances have meaning by nature. Yet such an argument is not immediately persuasive. After all, the sounds made by animals seem to have meaning. Such meaning can have no origin other than nature. Aristotle peremptorily dismisses such an objection by denying that sounds of this sort are nouns. But such a response implies tacit acceptance of the proposition that the sounds made by animals do have meaning by nature, and Averroes therefore tries to explain that possibility.

He contends that the sounds which naturally have meaning for animals are discernible to us because they are composed of the same syllables as the ones we use in the utterances we voice or because they are composed of syllables which seem to be similar to the letters we use.[9] Yet that explanation only tells us why we recognize the sounds used by animals as having some kind of meaning. It tells us nothing about why they actually do have meaning. Since man alone possesses reason, such sounds cannot have meaning because animals consciously imitate human sounds. Nor can the meaning in these sounds be explained in terms of onomatopoeia, for such sounds are imitative, not significative. Unfortunately, Averroes says nothing more here about such sounds. He does not return to the problem until his discussion of the conventional character of the sentence.

Averroes is not content simply to repeat Aristotle's explanation that a sentence has meaning by convention rather than by nature. He insists on engaging in an attack upon those who contend that all meanings and utterances have

[9] See below, paras. 4-5 with Aristotle *De Interpretatione* 16^{a}20-29.

a natural basis, that we have no choice in our use of utterances but must seek to marry utterances and composite expressions with their natural meanings.[10] Yet, rather than seek to show why such a contention is erroneous, Averroes argues against it by restating his own conventionalist position. And he ties that restatement to Aristotle's earlier definition of the noun as a conventional utterance, a move that allows him to return to his earlier explanation of the similarity between human utterances and those animal sounds which seem to have meaning by nature. Now, however, he explains that similarity in terms of the equivocal use of the term "sound" and the term "utterance": only when these expressions are used equivocally can it be said that men use utterances which are similar to the ones animals use by nature. Although Averroes does not say so, there is a very good reason for confusion about these terms in Greek. Unlike Arabic, which has a separate term for sound (*ṣawt*) and for utterance (*lafẓ*), Greek has only one term (*phōnē*). Passing over this peculiarity in the two languages, even though he indicates other peculiarities in other parts of his commentary, Averroes restates his view that meaning in sentences or utterances—that is, how sentences and utterances originally come to signify something—is completely within man's choice, because it is entirely dependent upon convention. Again, he has not thereby explained why sounds have meaning by nature for animals, whereas only convention gives them meaning for men. He has only asserted this conventionalist position; he has not proven it. Nonetheless, the consequence of tracing the similarity between animal sounds and human utterances to equivocal speech is, in effect, a denial of the notion that animal sounds have meaning by nature. And such a denial is consistent with the view that man alone has reason.

Neither Aristotle nor Averroes embraces such a conventionalist position in order to deny that there is a natural order or that human thought should strive to fathom that order. To the contrary, both are most desirous of deter-

[10] See below, para. 15 with Aristotle *De Interpretatione* 17a1-2.

mining the conditions for pronouncing about the truth or falsehood of speech. This concern is intimately linked with their conviction that while men are free to shape speech as they wish, they should strive to make it reflect what really exists outside of the mind and not just any individual whim or fancy. Utterances as such do not admit of truth or falsehood. They must be combined or divided before truth or falsehood is applicable to them; that is, they must be used in such a way that a judgment is expressed. And the goal of this book is to discuss the declarative sentence, because it has truth and falsehood as primary attributes.[11] So once we have understood the basic elements of the sentence and have some awareness of what a sentence is, that is, what human beings intend to express by means of a sentence, we are ready to examine how sentences relate to one another and ultimately how they can be used to inform us about the world around us. Yet, since the only way we can discern all the different possible relations of the sentence is to pursue it in all of its technical possibilities and to seek its opposite or contrary in each instance, Averroes warns us that the examples used in the ensuing discussion will not necessarily conform to reality. He is much more concerned than Aristotle about clarifying this fictitious aspect of the discussion and draws our attention to it at some length on two occasions, whereas Aristotle deems it worth no more than a passing remark.[12] The point is that even though man determines how speech will function, how meaning will be expressed in utterances and sentences, the limits imposed by reality cannot be ignored. That is to say, they cannot be ignored unless one is willing to be reduced to speaking nonsense. In the real world, a world that is ordered, truth cannot contradict truth. Differently stated, the propositions and their opposites or contraries to be examined in what follows should be considered not as reflections of reality, but as examples of how utterances may be combined.

[11] See below, paras. 3 and 11 with Aristotle *De Interpretatione* 16ª10-19 and 17ª5-8.

[12] See below, paras. 21 and 95 with Aristotle *De Interpretatione* 24ª6-7.

III

This question of the relationship between the real world and the kinds of things that can be imagined comes into sharper focus in the second chapter of Averroes' commentary, a chapter that corresponds to Aristotle's chapters 7-9. Averroes begins by thoroughly enumerating the six different classes of opposite propositions that can be formed by taking the subject universally or particularly and with or without a particle that indicates its quality. Of the six classes enumerated, only three are discussed by Aristotle. He says nothing about the others. In other words, Averroes introduces classes of opposite propositions that were not presented by Aristotle. He does not explain how he arrives at these additional classes and is content simply to list all of their possible combinations. Then, following this same detailed enumeration, Averroes identifies the instances in which both of the statements paired in opposite propositions may be true or both false and the instances in which one being true necessitates that the other be false.[13] This discussion is very important as a preface to the explanation of the principle of contradiction and that, in turn, for the larger argument about whether contingency exists.

To ask whether contingency exists is simply another way of asking whether future things are possible rather than necessary. The question occurs because it is obvious that of two opposing statements about past or present matters, one must be true and the other false. Socrates either existed or did not exist, and the man over there in the corner with a white hat on his head is either standing or is not standing. While no objection can be brought against such an understanding of statements concerning past and present matters, what is the case with future matters? If the same holds of two statements concerning future matters, that is, one must be true and the other false, then nothing can exist by chance. At this point, Aristotle's explanation becomes so turbulent that it is nearly impossible to follow his line of

[13] See below, paras. 23-24 with Aristotle *De Interpretatione* 17ᵇ5-18ᵃ7.

thought. Averroes, however, remains very lucid and carefully follows out all of the steps of the problem.[14]

Admitting the strangeness of the conclusion that nothing
exists by chance, Averroes tries to show that it is nonetheless
a more appealing notion than its contrary, namely, that
things may happen in just any way at all. Since to argue
that things must either necessarily exist or not exist in the
future depends on supposing that things can exist only in
a determinate manner, such a presupposition is far less
potentially disastrous than attempting to imagine a world
in which things would be both true and not true or would
be neither true nor not true. Yet there is something patently
absurd about this whole series of arguments, as Averroes
alone points out. Above all, it depends upon a complete
abstraction from practical life. Although he did not say as
much, Aristotle must have recognized the same problem,
for he, like Averroes, pauses in order to consider the problematic consequences of the argument against chance and
to note that it leaves no room at all for human deliberation.
Upon reflection, it now seems reasonable to argue that even
though one of two things must necessarily be or not be, it
can be affected by any number of other things—above all,
by human interference. If so, its existence is not necessary,
but contingent. Things necessarily do or do not exist, but
we cannot know beforehand whether a particular thing will
or will not come to be nor even when it might come to be.

Now this argument from practical experience does no
more than confirm our belief in the efficacy of human will.
It does not prove that things really do exist according to
contingency. We see, to be sure, that unbridled reason leads
to conclusions about future things that have unacceptable
practical consequences. Therefore, the conclusions of unbridled reason have to be modified. At this point Aristotle
introduces an example of a coat that may wear out before
it is cut apart. Averroes takes up the same example and
follows Aristotle in explaining that before the fact, we cannot know which will happen. Although it is clear that some-

---

[14] See below, paras. 28-38 with Aristotle *De Interpretatione* 18ª28-19ᵇ4.

thing will happen to the coat, we do not know what. Yet this does not depend on human will. Nor is it by any means a matter for deliberation. In other words, there are matters of contingency which lie outside the realm of the human will.

The immediate consequence of this argument is the recognition by both authors that the realm of the possible and the necessary needs to be carefully distinguished. Now Averroes becomes far more precise and loquacious than Aristotle. He painstakingly explains the three different categories of the possible and the two different categories of the necessary, along with all of the subdivisions of the latter. Apparently his tongue is loosened because of his concern about the relationship between these matters of contingency and the question of prophecy. Indeed, in the course of his explanation, he stresses that what is said must conform to the way things exist in the world around us and then goes on to point out that there is room here for the foretelling of future events. Things which are literally possible for the most part (*mumkin ʿalā al-akthar*), that is to say, probable, are such that we may know about their coming to be before that actually occurs. And though Averroes does not say so explicitly, this would appear to be the realm of prophecy.

These reflections also lead to another question which he could not have failed to notice, even though he says nothing about it: God's knowledge of particulars. If things do not exist of necessity, if they may exist in one way or another depending upon other factors that cannot be determined beforehand, then they are not foreordained. Differently stated, God's knowledge of particulars does not determine their coming into being or passing away ahead of time. Such things appear to belong to the second category of necessity as defined by Averroes, namely, things whose existence or non-existence is necessary in the moment in which they do or do not exist. Yet his explanation of this category of necessity is so abstract that it is difficult to see how it applies to particulars. As though he wishes to avoid such precision, Averroes keeps his explanation at a level of universals—man and reason. As a result, the elements of the discussion approach the fringes of grave philosophical questions, but do not go beyond. And in a way that is only fitting, for the primary purpose of the discussion is to explain the elements of rational discourse. The application of rational discourse to such important questions is truly the subject of another inquiry.

IV

Now that the six different kinds of opposite propositions have been enumerated and the way their affirmations or denials relate to truth and falsehood explained, it is appropriate to investigate these propositions as propositions and to determine how some imply others. This is the subject of Averroes' third chapter, and his discussion loosely corresponds to Aristotle's chapters 10 and 11. It corresponds insofar as each of the two major divisions in Averroes' third chapter encompasses precisely the subjects treated in each of Aristotle's respective chapters. But this correspondence must be described as a loose one, because Averroes adapts Aristotle's exposition to the needs of the Arabic language without bothering to indicate the ways in which such an adaptation requires him to depart from that exposition. Moreover, his extensive reliance on later commentators throughout this portion of the commentary, a reliance at no point explicitly acknowledged, renders the correspondence between the two texts even looser.

Nonetheless, Averroes' unusual approach succeeds in making Aristotle's text clearer and more orderly. Whereas Aristotle begins with an account of the affirmative proposition and moves to an enumeration of all the other possible kinds of propositions, without any apparent order or purpose, Averroes proceeds according to a very fixed schema. First, relying upon Aristotle's acknowledgement that the verb "is" in the phrase "man is just" constitutes a third term in the sentence, Averroes follows the lead of the commentators and distinguishes between binary and ternary propositions. Binary propositions are those in which the predicate is a verb or, differently stated, those in which the predicate is not related to the subject by means of the verb. Ternary propositions are those composed of a predicate and a subject which are nouns, as well as of a verb which relates the predicate to the subject. Having made this distinction, Averroes then speculates about the number of different kinds of binary and ternary propositions which can be formed when their negations and affirmations are combined with the six different kinds of opposites and these in turn with the three different tenses of the verb. Such speculation leads to the discovery that 216 binary propositions and twice as many ternary propositions can be found.[15] He says nothing about the significance of arriving at such a determination. Nor, apart from the fact that the reader who bothers to work out every possibility thereby acquires a good idea of how propositions are formed, is any significance immediately evident.

The reason that ternary propositions are two times more numerous than binary propositions is that they allow for the indefinite predicate. Thus, whereas sentences of the form "man not-is, not-man not-is" cannot be formulated, sentences of the sort "man is not-just, not-man is not-just" can be formulated. These latter kinds of sentences, along with their negations, are called retractive sentences and are distinguished from simple sentences of the sort "man is just, not-man is just" and their negations.[16] Having made these distinctions, Averroes turns to a very elaborate explanation of the relationship between affirmative and negative simple sentences, affirmative and negative retractive sentences, and affirmative and negative privative sentences—that is, sentences of the sort "man is unjust, man is not unjust." Although the basic schema corresponds slightly to part of Aristotle's discussion, the conclusions Averroes draws about the way these sentences do or do not necessarily imply each other have no parallel in Aristotle's text.[17]

[15] See below, paras. 40-41 with Aristotle *De Interpretatione* 19ᵇ22-23 and 19ᵇ5-19.
[16] See below, paras. 40-41 with paras. 42 and 48.
[17] See below, paras. 42-46.

Averroes seems intent upon showing how these sentences relate to each other as sentences and upon drawing our attention to the fact that they cannot truly relate to each other unless they tell us something about the world around us. He continues to think about the admonition set down at the beginning of the book to the effect that meanings are connnected with the way things are. And to ensure that no one misses that point, he explains the soundness of each of his examples.

Before citing one or two of these provocative examples, an apparent contradiction should probably be addressed: there is no conflict between this observation that Averroes requires his sentences to tell us something about the world around us and his earlier explanation that many of the sentences used in the treatise do not reflect reality. The point is that thorough investigation demands an examination of every possibility, and this leads to the formulation of sentences that negate patently true sentences or affirm patently false sentences. Such opposite or contrary sentences have nothing to do with reality. They are enumerated simply for the sake of thorough investigation. In reality, they utter nonsense. Other sentences are true and do conform to reality. These are the ones worth reflecting about in order to understand the world around us better.

For example, even though an affirmative simple sentence of the order "man is just" necessarily gives rise to the negative retractive sentence "man is not not-just," the converse does not hold. The reason is that this latter sentence can be asserted not only of the just man, but also of the person to whom neither justice nor injustice is attributed, that is, of the child or of the non-citizen. In terms of logic, then, the negative retractive sentence is more general than the affirmative simple sentence. This much Averroes clearly explains.[18] In terms of ethics, a little reflection leads to the consideration that a person must be old enough to be capable of rational and responsible action before it is appropriate to speak of him or her in terms of justice or injustice.

---

[18] See below, para. 43.

Similarly, such terms have no meaning for anyone who is not a citizen, because justice and injustice are primarily related to living under the rule of law with others. In other words, there is no such thing as justice or injustice in the state of nature. Such a conclusion does not necessarily imply that there is no such thing as a natural standard of justice or natural right, for it is always possible that recognition of such a standard requires a high level of intellectual achievement which in turn requires a developed polity. But to pursue such questions on such flimsy evidence is temerarious.

Averroes also notes that whereas an affirmative retractive sentence of the order "man is not-just" necessarily gives rise to the negative simple sentence "man is not just," the converse does not hold. His reasoning is similar to that used in the first case: the negative simple sentence has a broader application than the affirmative retractive sentence. In other words, the former applies to both the simply unjust person as well as to the person who is not described in terms either of justice or of injustice—that is, again the child or the non-citizen—whereas the latter applies only to the unjust person. Here, too, the logical point is as obvious as the ethical implication. To make the implication even more patent, Averroes patiently explains that to speak of someone as "not-just" is to speak in terms of a privation, and privation, as defined in the *Categories*, refers to the absence of what ought to exist in someone at the time it ought to exist.[19] Blindness in human beings is a usual example of privation; baldness is another. In other words, justice is fundamental to human existence; its absence at the time it ought to exist is as much a privation as the loss of sight or hair. But since it clearly is not a usual attribute of the child or the non-citizen, when ought it to exist? Apparently, it is proper to the rational and mature individual who lives under a regime of laws. But once again,

[19] See below, para. 44; also above, *Middle Commentary on Aristotle's Categories*, paras. 92 and 97.

to take these speculations any further would be to go beyond the limits of the text.

Averroes presents a more faithful interpretation of Aristotle's remarks in the rest of this chapter. These remarks constitute a clear break with what has preceded and correspond to Aristotle's discussion of how to select predicates correctly, a discussion presented in his own chapter 11. Unless predicates are selected correctly, a sentence will have more than one meaning and thus lead to confusion. This is particularly important in dialectical questioning and answering, and both authors take special pains to indicate how dialectical questions should be formulated. In this context, Aristotle refers to the *Topics* as a work he has already written. Averroes goes even further and draws the reader's attention to a specific passage in the *Topics* or in his middle commentary on that work.[20] Whatever position one wishes to take with respect to the debate about the date of composition of Aristotle's works, Averroes' remark is significant for the question of when his own works were composed. Although one of the two known Arabic manuscripts of his middle commentary on the *Topics* does contain a date explaining when the second part of that work was finished and both of the known Arabic manuscripts of his middle commentary on the *Rhetoric* contain dates explaining when that commentary was finished, nothing more is known about when he wrote these works or in what order he wrote them. However, it is significant to note that in his middle commentary on the *Topics* he refers to the other logical works in terms of what Aristotle said or set forth in them, whereas in this treatise as well as in his middle commentaries on the other logical works he refers to what was explained in each work. In other words, whereas the references in his middle commentary on the *Topics* are clearly to Aristotle's works and to Aristotle's discussion in those works, his references in these other middle commentaries can as readily be understood as references to his own writings as to Aristotle's. And this would suggest that Averroes first composed

---

[20] See below, paras. 57-58 and Aristotle *De Interpretatione* 20ᵇ14-26.

his middle commentary on the *Topics* and then composed these other middle commentaries.

Yet another way in which Averroes diverges from Aristotle in this section is worth noting. When discussing how dialectical questions ought to be formulated, Aristotle criticizes Socrates indirectly by insisting that the question "what is it" (*to ti estin*) is not a dialectical question.[21] Averroes takes that criticism as an invitation to distinguish between dialectical and didactical questioning. Like Aristotle, he refrains from mentioning Socrates by name. But in handling Aristotle's muted criticism in such a fashion, he offers his own appreciation of what Socrates sought to achieve as a dialectician. For Averroes, Socrates was above all a teacher with a particular point of view. He thus thinks that Socrates used dialectic in order to instruct others, not in order to investigate things of which he was ignorant. Differently stated, Averroes understands Socratic dialectic to be more the didactic formulation of arguments already pursued by means of another logical art than a tool of disinterested inquiry. Even though he pursues the matter no further here, these remarks are significant because they correspond so closely to the appreciation of dialectic he brings forth in his *Middle Commentary on Aristotle's Topics*.

V

Averroes' fourth chapter, like Aristotle's chapters 12 and 13, is concerned with modal propositions and the relationships existing between them. Modal propositions affirm or deny the possible, contingent, impossible, or necessary relationship of a subject to a predicate. The relationship existing between these kinds of propositions—that is, the way some modal propositions imply or are opposed to others—are numerous, and both of our authors find the explanation of these relationships to be fraught with difficulties. This is especially true with respect to modal sentences indicating the possible and those indicating the necessary, for the

[21] See below, para. 59 with Aristotle *De Interpretatione* 20b27-30.

different meanings attached to each term oblige both Aristotle and Averroes to set forth long and painstaking explanations of how the two are related. Throughout his commentary on this section of the text, Averroes patiently details each step of his explanation and thereby goes beyond Aristotle's text even to the point of embarking upon discussions never broached by Aristotle.

For example, in the very first paragraph of the fourth chapter, Averroes explains that there are two kinds of modal utterances: one denotes the necessary and what follows upon it, while the other denotes the possible and what follows upon it. Then, in order to make sure that his division of modal propositions into the necessary and the possible is readily understood, he explains that such a division is warranted because there are two divisions of existence—potential and actual. We speak of what is actually in existence in terms of the necessary and of what is potentially existent in terms of the possible. Now these are remarks having no parallel in Aristotle's text. And, as though to compensate for this addition, Averroes omits Aristotle's discussion of modal propositions concerned with contingency. Although he does speak in passing of the contingent as that which follows upon the possible, just as he speaks of the impossible as that which is necessarily non-existent, he omits all mention of contingent modal sentences from the rest of his discussion and limits himself to an account of those sentences which are concerned with the necessary, the impossible, and the possible. Moreover, in this first paragraph, Averroes is far more precise than Aristotle about the way the following discussion will be organized. From the very outset, he explains that his account will center around an investigation of the opposites of modal sentences and of their consequences, both with respect to retractive modal sentences and to simple modal sentences.[22] Although Aristotle does discuss the opposites of modal sentences in chapter 12 and their consequences in chapter 13,

[22] See below, paras. 65-68 with Aristotle *De Interpretatione* 21ᵃ38-22ᵃ9.

the reader is given no indication that the first discussion is intimately linked to the second.

Nonetheless, Averroes does offer much the same account as Aristotle of the way the opposites of modal sentences should be formulated. This subject deserves to be treated at some length because of genuine doubt about where the negative particle should be placed in such sentences. For example, when formulating the opposite of a simple affirmative modal sentence—that is, when formulating a simple negative modal sentence—should the negative particle be placed with the existential verb or with the predicate or elsewhere? In other words, what is the opposite of the proposition "it is possible that man is just"? If we place the negative particle with the existential verb and say "it is possible that man is not just," we have not formulated an opposite proposition. Indeed, that proposition is simply a fuller explanation of the meaning of what is possible. For if something may possibly exist, it may possibly not exist. Otherwise, its existence would be necessary rather than possible. Yet we clearly cannot place the negative particle with the predicate and say "it is possible that man is not-just," for that sentence also represents a fuller explanation of the meaning of the possible rather than its opposite. And it is an example of a retractive affirmative modal sentence, not of a negative simple modal sentence. Thus the only way to formulate the opposite of an affirmative modal proposition is to place the negative particle with the modal inflection. Here, then, the opposite of the sentence "it is possible that man is just" would be the sentence "it is not possible that man is just."[23] Averroes' lengthy and involved discussion of what at first seems to be a minor point shows clearly how difficult it actually is to arrive at a correct formulation of the modal negative and thus establishes the relevance of this issue for the ensuing discussion.

Although he does reach conclusions similar to Aristotle's with respect to the consequences of modal sentences, the steps of his account differ greatly. Whereas Aristotle lists

[23] See below, paras. 69-70 with Aristotle *De Interpretatione* 22ᵃ14-32.

the kinds of consequences to which modal sentences give rise and then arranges four of these sentences with three of their consequences in a four-part table, Averroes begins by identifying four different kinds of modal sentences as well as two consequences for each kind and then places these sentences into a table consisting of six sentences and their six opposites. Aristotle's explanation has four more sentences than Averroes' because it allows for contingent sentences. Nonetheless, Averroes' discussion is technically far more precise than Aristotle's. He first identifies each of his twelve sentences according to the terms he set forth earlier in the commentary—that is, as affirmative or negative simple possible, affirmative or negative retractive possible, affirmative or negative simple necessary, affirmative or negative retractive necessary, affirmative or negative simple impossible, and affirmative or negative retractive impossible—and then he provides an example of each sentence. Consequently, when he arranges these sentences according to a table or diagram, it is easier to follow his explanation. But while the reasons for these divergences from Aristotle are patent, the considerations which prompted him to reverse Aristotle's arrangement of the necessary and impossible modal sentences remain obscure.

At any rate, consistent use of precise terminology also allows Averroes to explain very clearly a problem that arises with respect to the consequences of necessary sentences. Before touching upon that problem, he and Aristotle note that contradictories are the consequences of impossible and possible sentences. That is to say, an affirmative possible sentence of the order "it is possible that he exists" has as its consequence a negative impossible sentence of the order "it is not impossible that he exists." Similarly, an affirmative impossible sentence of the order "it is impossible that he exists" has a negative possible sentence of the order "it .is not possible that he exists" as a consequence.[24] But both Aristotle and Averroes note with some consternation that matters are by no means so simple with respect to necessary

[24] See below, para. 71 with Aristotle *De Interpretatione* 22ª33-37.

sentences. As Averroes explains it, a necessary sentence gives rise to a contrary of a contradictory sentence, not simply to a contradictory sentence. Both offer very complex explanations of this anomaly, but the major point is that because of the numerous ways in which the word possible is used, difficulty arises whenever we attempt to speak of the possible sentences to which necessary sentences give rise. Logical analysis does not help to clarify the problem, and Averroes even finds himself forced to admit that his table has been constructed wrongly. In the end, each of our authors concludes that his explanation actually proves the soundness of beginning a discussion of the consequences of modal sentences with an examination of the consequences of necessary sentences.[25]

Averroes embellishes the discussion somewhat by presenting a demonstrative proof for his contention that the consequence, with respect to necessary modalities, of the affirmative simple possible sentence "it is possible that he exists" is the negative retractive necessary sentence "it is not necessary that he not-exist." His demonstration consists of an enumeration of all the kinds of necessary sentences to which the affirmative simple possible sentence could give rise—that is, the negative simple, the affirmative simple, the affirmative retractive, and the negative retractive—and a careful examination of each of those sentences. Then he eliminates all but the negative retractive necessary sentence and explains why it indeed constitutes a consequence.[26] He closes the discussion by twice indicating that he is about to quote Aristotle, but the phrase following *qāl* (he said) is not from Aristotle's text. The first of these two non-quotations simply allows Averroes to point to the conclusion of the preceding discussion in a more forceful manner than Aristotle had done, and the second allows him to indicate that these questions will be discussed at greater length in the book which follows *De Interpretatione*, namely, the *Prior Analytics*.

[25] See below, paras. 72-83 with Aristotle *De Interpretatione* 22ª38-23ª17.
[26] See below, paras. 82-83 with Aristotle *De Interpretatione* 23ª18-27.

VI

Both Aristotle and Averroes deem the problem of determining the real contrary of a given sentence worth a single chapter and both devote the final chapters of their treatises to this question. However, unlike the procedure each has followed in earlier chapters, here it is Aristotle who moves directly and concisely to a resolution of the problem, whereas Averroes is the one to engage in discussions and speculations which are more confusing than illuminating. The problem arises because almost any given proposition can be countered by a negation or by means of a second affirmative proposition which is contrary to the original proposition. To take the example used by both Aristotle and Averroes, it is possible to counter the proposition "every man is just" by the negation "no man is just" or by the contrary proposition "every man is unjust." Given such a proposition, it is not immediately evident which of these latter two kinds of sentences is most contrary to the original sentence.

Aristotle defends the merit of this investigation on the grounds that we do not always form an intellectual judgment which corresponds to the judgment expressed in a contrary proposition. Were it possible to be confident that we would always understand how thoroughly a contrary sentence destroys the thrust of the sentence it counters, no valid problem would arise. However, we sometimes fail to seize the significance of the contrary sentence, that is, to perceive that it is contrary to the original sentence. And in some instances, what seems to be a contrary sentence does not actually express a contrary judgment. Thus, although the proposition that death is bad is opposed to the proposition that life is good, they are not contrary propositions. Both are true propositions, whereas contrary propositions are such that one must be true and the other false.[27]

Even though he addresses himself to the same problem as Aristotle, Averroes places that problem within the context of the preceding discussion. Rather than present it as

27 See ibid., 23ª28-23ᵇ7.

yet another question arising from reflection about language but whose significance can be proven, Averroes reminds the reader of what has already been established in earlier parts of the treatise and states the issue in terms of what we believe to be most contrary. He first reminds the reader of the earlier discussion of opposites and maintains the distinction set forth there between sentences concerned with partial or individual meanings and those concerned with general meanings, for the present problem involves only the latter kinds of opposites. In this context, he stresses the beliefs we hold about contrary propositions and thereby creates the impression that he, too, thinks the problem arises primarily because we may form faulty judgments about them. However, as though he were not content to state the problem solely in these terms, Averroes then proceeds to revise Aristotle's explanation of the possibility that our intellectual judgments may not conform to the sense of the judgments we utter in speech and makes the issue turn on which kind of proposition is more likely to compel our assent. He takes as a premise the argument set forth at the very beginning of the commentary about the way our utterances correspond to the meanings in our souls and goes on to ask whether belief in the contrary of a given proposition or belief in its negation is greater. In other words, the problem posed by Averroes is anchored in the way the workings of language have been set forth thus far, not in the possible disparity between speech and mental perception.[28]

However, to formulate the problem in this fashion is to formulate it incorrectly. Even though what we believe to be contrary resembles what really is contrary, our beliefs are so numerous that the correspondence between belief and fact does not always hold. Speaking in his own name and without reference to Aristotle's text, Averroes admits this disparity. Such an admission does not prompt him to bring the statement of the problem back to Aristotle's formulation, but rather to discover the roots of the disparity

---

[28] See below, paras. 85-86 with paras. 2 and 23.

and then to explain what permits us to have an absolute belief that a given proposition is indeed contrary to another one.[29] Only at this point does his argument rejoin Aristotle's.

Like Aristotle, Averroes thinks that the negative sentence stands most fully as the contrary of a given proposition. He does not deny that many beliefs and sentences may be contrary to a given sentence, but he does insist that only one belief and sentence stand forth as being contrary without question. The negative sentence is an essential, self-evident contrary. That is to say, whereas it is necessary to go through a series of logical steps in order to understand why the sentence "every man is unjust" represents the contrary of the sentence "every man is just," it is immediately clear why the sentence "no man is just" stands as its contrary. Or, as Averroes says by way of further illustration, non-existence is more contrary to existence than any of the other kinds of contrary states such as coming into being or passing away. Non-existence, or the privation of existence, is more contrary because it partakes in no way of existence. Both of these other contraries do partake of it, even if only accidentally. And insofar as a negation completely removes the force of the affirmative sentence, it represents an essential contrary. What is more, it can be brought forward as a contrary even with respect to those beliefs and sentences that otherwise have no contrary.[30]

Having established that the negative sentence is the most complete contrary of an affirmative sentence, Aristotle attempts to conclude his argument by showing that the converse is also true. The point here is that the relation between affirmation and negation constitutes the basic contrary. Averroes follows Aristotle's explanation in all of its details and enriches it somewhat by elaborating why each of the other possibilities does not represent a contrary. Then both authors conclude the discussion by explaining that the contrary relation is in no way affected if the affirmation is cast

[29] See below, paras. 87-89 and Aristotle *De Interpretatione* 23ᵇ8-14.
[30] See below, paras. 90-91 and Aristotle *De Interpretatione* 23ᵇ15-32.

in universal terms. In his own more ample account of this point, Averroes is so persuaded by the foregoing explanation that he reformulates his own terminology. He now thoroughly identifies the negative sentence as the only proper contrary and seems to forget that there are other instances of the contrary. Thus, when explaining how the universal negation of a universal affirmative sentence is formulated, he speaks of this negation as the contrary and thereby relegates the more usual notion of contrary to oblivion. According to his remarks in earlier passages, the contrary of the sentence "every man is good" should be "every man is not good." The reason is that a contrary is formulated by modifying the predicate of the sentence. Here, however, Averroes offers "not one man is good" as the contrary. And he does so even though it is actually an instance of a negation.[31]

The basic logical point now having been firmly established, both Aristotle and Averroes remind the reader that these references to contraries have definite limits. Of two contrary propositions, one must be true and the other false. The reason is, in Averroes' words: "it is not possible that one truth be contrary to another, nor that one true belief be contrary to another, nor that one utterance be contradictory of another when both signify an idea which is in itself true." He then goes on to explain that contrary beliefs are to be found only in certain kinds of sentences whose affirmation and denial constitute opposites. Even though Aristotle was content to leave these final remarks with the assertion that two contraries cannot come together in the same subject, Averroes calls the reader's attention to the earlier discussion of this problem and then enumerates the kinds of sentences that do admit contraries.[32] He does not thereby alter Aristotle's argument or skew it in any way, but he does make the point more explicit and remind the reader that it has already been discussed. Thus, at the very end of his commentary, just as in its earlier parts, he re-

[31] See below, paras. 92-93; also para. 94 with paras. 71-73 and 78. See also Aristotle *De Interpretatione* 23ᵇ33-24ᵇ6.

[32] See below, paras. 95 and 24 with Aristotle *De Interpretatione* 24ᵇ7-9.

mains faithful to his goal of making Aristotle's allusions explicit and of providing detailed explanations of Aristotle's otherwise laconic utterances.

VII

In this sense, Averroes serves as a worthy interpreter of Aristotle's treatise. He teaches us how to read this work and alerts us to problems we might otherwise neglect. His incessant concern for thorough explanation leads him to draw out the implications of Aristotle's remarks and to indicate how the different parts of the treatise fit together. His awareness of the tradition of commentary on Aristotle's text permits him to extend some of Aristotle's remarks, but does not lead him to misconstrue them or otherwise to draw conclusions Aristotle would have repudiated. To the contrary, the liberties Averroes permits himself with Aristotle's text contribute to the fuller interpretation of that text and to an appreciation of its comprehensive account of how language works.

There are, nonetheless, a number of questions which he never satisfactorily resolves. For example, although it is evident that Aristotle's remarks about the way language provides meaning for someone versed in Greek can be made clear to one who is versed in Arabic and that all of this can be grasped by one whose tongue is English, no clear account of the interaction between language, nature, and convention is ever provided. We note that it is possible to speak across linguistic traditions about the conventions which govern them and we accept the assertion that we all perceive the same natural beings, however we might express those beings and their relationships in our different linguistic traditions, but we never encounter here a full explanation of how we come to have this common image. Similarly, even though we leave this commentary with a clearer understanding of how to formulate propositions and with a greater awareness of the various relationships between our propositions, we do not really understand why those relationships are sound. Averroes has explained what

Aristotle said about those relationships and he has fully developed Aristotle's remarks, but he has not proven their soundness. Nor has he indicated their significance. Although the ultimate purpose of knowing how each of these propositions is opposed to others or how each implies others must surely be to enable us to formulate more clearly the premises of syllogisms, almost nothing is said by our commentator about the way the teaching presented here provides for that presented in the *Prior Analytics*. Nor, with the exception of his references here to the remarks about privation in the *Categories*, is any attempt made to link the teaching of that work with the teaching of this one.

There are also some questions which one would have desired Averroes to address, even though they are not raised by Aristotle. Despite obvious problems with his account of the principle of contradiction, Aristotle maintains that it must be kept as a principle. Averroes modifies Aristotle's account enough to provide for the existence of future contingencies and for the difficulties surrounding the relationships between possible and necessary sentences, but he leaves the principle intact. An explanation of why he does this would allow us to appreciate the principle more fully. Similarly, an explanation of why he accepts the terminology of the commentators and classifies Aristotle's sentences as binary or ternary would help us to understand how he uses those commentators and what he considers their merit to be. And it would be helpful to have a more adequate explanation of why some opposite sentences are not always opposite. Averroes provides the beginnings of such an explanation by his account of how each of the different parts of opposite sentences does or does not function as an opposition, but he never goes beyond such an enumeration to examine why this occurs.

Still, it may be unfair to criticize Averroes for failing to clarify problems left obscure by Aristotle or for his reluctance to introduce questions Aristotle never raised. After all, he stated his goal to be only that of explaining Aristotle's teaching; he nowhere claimed that he intended to improve upon that teaching. Moreover, his commentary bears ample witness to the thoughtful simplicity we have come to associate with classical writings. It raises more problems than it solves, precisely because it causes us to think along with the author. Thus Averroes and Aristotle both provide us with the elements for answering the question about the interaction between nature, language, and convention without actually providing us with an answer. Both show us how language is guided by convention and both lead us to think about how it reflects the natural order. But neither states explicitly how language comes to reflect that order, because such a statement depends upon further inquiry into nature and into the human soul. Yet even though neither of them speaks to that problem here, both insist that such inquiry will reveal the correspondence because both are persuaded that the human soul can perceive the natural order. That is to say, both Aristotle and Averroes think that man can understand the world he lives in not only because he has the mental capacity to do so, but also because the world is such as to be comprehensible. Here, however, both of our authors limit themselves to discussing the tools by which we can pursue that task: sentences, the nouns and verbs of which they are composed, and the various ways they imply or counter other sentences.

THE ORDER OF THE ARGUMENT

THE TEXT

CHAPTER ONE

1. He said: we ought first to say what a noun and   16ª1-3
verb are. Then, after that, we will say what affirmation
and negation are and, in general, what the judgment
and the sentence, which is the genus of affirmation
and negation, are.

2. Thus, we say that spoken utterances signify pri-   16ª4-9
marily the ideas that are in the soul, while written letters signify primarily these utterances. Just as written
letters—I mean, script—are not one and the same for
all nations, so too, the utterances by which ideas are
expressed are not one and the same for all nations.
Therefore, the meaning of both script and spoken
utterances[1] comes from convention rather than nature.
And the ideas which are in the soul are one and the
same for all people, just as the beings which the ideas
in the soul are examples of and signify are one and
exist by nature for all people. But to speak about the
way the ideas in the soul signify the external beings
belongs to a science other than this one. It has been
discussed[2] in the De Anima.

3. Utterances resemble the ideas that are intellected   16ª10-19
in that just as something is sometimes intellected without having truth or falsehood attributed to it, so too,
an utterance is sometimes understood without having
truth or falsehood attributed to it. And just as what is
intellected about something sometimes has truth or

[1] Literally, "both of these" or "these two" (hādhaini).

[2] Or "he discussed it," Aristotle being the implied subject of the
verb. The immediately following reference may be to De Anima
III.iii.427ª17-vii.431ᵇ19.

falsehood attributed to it, so too, what is understood about an utterance sometimes has truth or falsehood attributed to it. Truth and falsehood attach to the ideas that are intellected and to the utterances which signify them when some are combined with others or separated from others. When they are taken as uncombined, they signify neither truth nor falsehood. The noun and the verb resemble uncombined ideas which are neither true nor false, that is, the ones which are taken without being combined or separated. An example of that is our saying "man" and "whiteness." For as long as "exists" or "does not exist" is not joined to it, it is neither true nor false. Instead it signifies a designated thing, without that thing having truth or falsehood attributed to it. Therefore, neither truth nor falsehood can be attributed to our saying "goat-stag" and "griffon" unless "exists" or "does not exist" is joined to it—whether without qualification or according to a particular time—and we then say "a goat-stag is existent," "a goat-stag is not existent," or "a goat-stag exists or does not exist."

THE DISCUSSION OF THE NOUN

16ᵃ20-27   4. The noun is an utterance which, by convention, signifies an idea without reference to time; yet if one of its parts were taken as uncombined, it would not signify any part of that idea, whether the uncombined noun were simple—like "Zayd" or "'Amr"—or combined—like the "'Abd al-Malik" which is a man's name.[3] That is because when "'Abd" or "al-Malik" is removed from the combination "'Abd al-Malik" which is a man's name, neither one signifies any part of the idea they signify when taken together, as they do when in saying "'abd al-malik" we mean that he is a servant of the king; here, "servant" does signify one part of the idea

[3] The word 'Abd (servant) is in a genitive relation to al-Malik (the king) thus forming the proper name, something like our "Kingman" or the descriptive term "the king's servant."

signified by our saying "servant of the king," and "the king" likewise signifies one part of the idea. The difference between simple and combined nouns—like "ʿAbd Qais" and "Baʿalbak"[4]—is that a part of the simple noun, namely, one of the syllables which make up the noun, signifies nothing at all, neither essentially nor accidentally—like the "Z" of "Zayd." Whereas, when a part of the combined noun is removed from the combination, it only accidentally means something— like when someone whose name is "ʿAbd al-Malik" happens to be a servant of a king.

5. "By convention" was added to the definition of the noun, because the utterances people speak do not by nature signify anything—like many of the sounds spoken by animals, namely, sounds which are not written. Indeed, the sounds voiced by many animals are made up of the syllables which make up the utterances spoken by man or of syllables made up of letters which approximate them in expression, and in themselves they signify ideas among the animals.   16ᵃ28-29

6. Nouns are either definite or indefinite. The definite noun is the one that signifies states—like "man" and "horse." The indefinite noun is the one that is composed of the name of the state and the particle[5] "not-" in those languages which use this kind of noun— like our saying "not-man" and "not-animal." This sort of noun is called indefinite because it does not deserve to be called a noun in an absolute sense: it does not   16ᵃ30-34

---

[4] In Arabic, *Baʿalbak* is a combination of two nouns, *Baʿal* and *Bak*, both of Chaldaean origin. Since *Baʿal* means lord or master and ultimately came to signify a local deity or idol among the ancient Semitic peoples, *Baʿalbak* refers to the deity or idol of the people of Bekka in Syria. Similarly, *ʿAbd Qais* is a combination of two nouns, *ʿAbd*, which has the meaning of servant referred to earlier in the paragraph as well as immediately hereafter, and *Qais*, which is the name of an Arabic tribe as well as a word for the male sexual organ or for famine. However, the combination *ʿAbd Qais* has no significance.

[5] The word translated here as "particle" (*ḥarf*) is the same word which is usually translated as "letter."

signify any state nor, insofar as it has the meaning of an uncombined noun even when it is combined, is it a negative sentence; therefore, just as with the definite noun, this one may be negated.

16ᵇ1-5   7. Moreover, when a noun is put into the accusative or genitive case or altered in some similar way, it is not said to be a noun in an absolute sense, but an inflected noun. Then again, some nouns are inflected and others uninflected. The definition set down for the noun encompasses both of these. Nonetheless, the difference between the inflected noun and the uninflected noun—which, in the speech of the Arabs, is the noun in the nominative case—is that if to the inflected nouns—which are also called declined nouns—something like "was" or "is" or "is now" is added and it is said "was Zayd" in the accusative or "is Zayd" in the genitive,⁶ they will be neither true nor false. The uninflected noun—which is called the sound noun—becomes true or false when one of these is added to it—like our saying in the nominative case "Zayd was" or "Zayd existed."

8. This is what he mentioned with respect to the definition of the noun and its sorts.

THE DISCUSSION OF THE VERB

16ᵇ6-12   9. The verb (*kalimah*), which the Arab grammarians call *fi'l*,⁷ is an utterance that signifies an idea and one of the three times by which that idea is defined—that is, the past, the present, or the future. Moreover, it is of the essence of the verb that none of its parts has meaning when uncombined. A particular character-

---

⁶ These two examples (*Zaydan kān, Zaydin yakūn*) cannot be imitated in English.

⁷ The two words are synonymous, but with rare exceptions Averroes uses the term *kalimah* throughout this text. The same distinction is made by al-Fārābī: "verbs (*al-kalim*) are what the Arab grammarians call *al-af'āl*." See *Kitāb al-Alfāẓ al-Musta'malah fī al-Manṭiq (The Book of Utterances Employed in Logic)*, ed. M. Mahdi (Beirut: Imprimerie Catholique, 1968), para. 1.

istic of the verb is that it is always what informs, not what is informed about, and is a predicate, not a subject. Therefore, it always signifies an idea which is such as to be predicated of another. This is so either when its form is such as to signify the predicated idea and the link between the predicate and the subject, which happens when it informs by itself—like your saying "Zayd is healthy" and "Zayd is walking"—or when its form is such as to signify the link between the predicate and the subject when the predicate is one of the nouns— like your saying "Zayd is an animal."[8] The predicate which signifies the link between itself and the subject is either that which is said about a subject—as when it is an accident of the subject—or that which is said of a subject—as when the predicate is part of the subject. The proviso added to the definition of the verb, that along with signifying an idea it signifies the time of that idea, is the differentia which distinguishes the verb from the noun. That is because our saying "is healthy," which is a verb, signifies what our saying "health," which is a noun, signifies and also signifies the present or future time in which health exists.[9]

10. Verbs, too, are definite and indefinite. The definite verb signifies the same idea as the definite noun and also the time of that idea. The indefinite verb signifies the same idea as the indefinite noun and also the time of that idea. The latter is the privation of what the definite noun signifies, that is, the privation defined in the *Categories*[10]—like our saying "was not healthy"— for it signifies what our saying "not-health" signifies and also signifies the time of that idea. The indefinite verb is one of the species of verb, since it falls under the preceding definition of the verb taken in an absolute sense and the preceding particular characteristic   16^b13-16

---

[8] Or, translating the verb *yūjad* according to the more literal sense given it in paras. 3 and 7, "Zayd exists as an animal."

[9] See below, para. 11.

[10] See above, *Middle Commentary on Aristotle's Categories*, paras. 92-93.

of the verb holds for it—namely, that it always signifies that which is such as to be predicated of something else, either predicating something of the subject or about the subject. This sort is called an indefinite verb only because it is derived from an indefinite noun. Yet just as with the indefinite noun, this species of verb does not exist in the Arabic language.

16ᵇ17-19   11. Some verbs are inflected and some are uninflected. The latter are the ones to which the name of verb applies in an absolute sense. The uninflected verb is the one which signifies present time in the language of many nations, and the inflected is the one which signifies the time which exists as though it revolves around present time—namely, past and future time. There is no particular form in the Arabic language for present time. In fact, the form for it in the speech of the Arabs is the same for the present and the future— like our saying "is healthy" and "is walking." Therefore the Arab grammarians say that when they want to stress a verb's future sense they add a *sīn* or *sawfa* to it and say "will be healthy" or "will be walking."¹¹ Present time is the one the mind takes as actually existing and as designated—like our saying "this hour" and "this moment." Therefore the name "time" is said of the present in an absolute sense, for it is best known to the multitude, and past and future time are understood in relation to it: the past precedes this time now, and the future comes after it. Whether or not what is imagined about present time exists the way it is imagined is not something that needs to be discussed in this place.

16ᵇ20-26   12. The verb resembles the noun and has something in common with it in that when said uncombined, a distinct idea may be understood in its own right—just as one may be understood from the noun when it is

¹¹ To the verb "is healthy" (*yaṣuḥḥ*) or "is walking" (*yamshī*), they add the letter *sīn*, thereby forming *sayaṣuḥḥ* or *sayamshī*; or they add the particle *sawfa*, thereby forming *sawfa yaṣuḥḥ* or *sawfa yamshī*. In both cases, the verbs have the force of the future.

said uncombined in its own right. Therefore when the hearer hears it, he is satisfied with it. However, the idea perceived by means of the verb provides no understanding about whether the thing exists yet or not—like our saying "was" or "is." This is the case when the verbs inform by themselves. But when they are linking verbs,[12] they provide no understanding about an idea which is distinct in itself—as is the case with the letter—because then they only signify the way the predicate is combined with the subject, and there is no way to understand that combination without understanding the things that are combined. The latter understanding occurs when these things are explicitly stated—like your saying "Zayd is learned" or "is not learned." So there are two sorts of verbs, a sort understood by itself—namely, the verbs which inform by themselves—and a sort not understood by itself—namely, the linking verbs,[12] which are called existential verbs.

13. This is what he said here about the definition of the noun and the verb[13] and about what it is necessary to know about their sorts, namely, the ones which produce different propositions. As for the particles, he speaks about them in the *Poetics*.[14]

THE DISCUSSION OF THE SENTENCE

14. The sentence is a significative utterance each 16ᵇ27-34 primary or simple part of which when uncombined signifies, insofar as it is an utterance, that it is an uncombined part, not that it is an affirmation or negation. An example of this is our saying "man is an animal," for the utterance "man," which is the first part of this sentence, signifies an uncombined thing, not whether that thing exists or not; and the same holds for the utterance "animal," which is the second part of this sentence. What has been included in the definition of

---

[12] That is, copulas.
[13] Here Averroes uses the term *fiʿl*. See above, para. 9, note 7.
[14] See Aristotle *Poetics* 1456ᵇ19-35.

the sentence about one of its primary parts signifying an uncombined idea is the differentia by which the sentence is distinguished from the noun. For none of the parts of the simple noun—namely, the syllables—signifies anything at all. Nor does any part of the combined noun signify anything, except by accident—like the man whose name is ʿAbd al-Malik happening to be a servant of a king.

17ª1-2   15. The sentence has meaning only by convention, not by nature nor in the sense that for every combined idea there is a combined utterance which naturally signifies it without this meaning existing in any other utterance, the way the function of an instrument exists in no other instrument. Now one group of people is of the opinion that the meaning of utterances is like this. Another group is of the opinion that utterances naturally have meaning without our having any choice at all about it—neither a choice in the way they are made up according to what is posited nor a choice in the way they are naturally made up. This is the opinion of those who hold that there are combinations of utterances here which naturally signify each and every idea. It might be said: "When Arisotle said in defining the noun, 'an utterance which signifies by convention,' this is what he meant."[15] But it might also be that by "utterance" he meant "sound," if one argues that ambiguity accounts for man and animal having utterances[16] in common—and this is the correct interpretation.

17ª5-8   16. Sentences are complete and incomplete. Some complete sentences are declarative and others not declarative—for example, command and prohibition. The goal here is only to discuss the declarative sentence. He speaks about complete sentences other than this in the *Rhetoric* and the *Poetics*, just as the other sorts of incomplete sentence—namely, definitions and general

[15] See above, para. 4, and Aristotle *De Interpretatione* 16ª20.
[16] The text has the singular.

descriptions—will be discussed in the *Posterior Analytics*.[17]

17. The declarative sentence is the one to which truth   17ª9-10
or falsehood is attributed. It is one of two sorts: simple
and combined. The simple is combined of one predicate and one subject, rather than of more than one
predicate and more than one subject. And it is of two
kinds. The first and prior kind is the affirmation, and
the second and subsequent kind is the negation.

18. It may be said of the sentence that it is single   17ª13-17
when it is a definition of one thing—like our saying of
man that he is a rational animal. However, this is an
idea about the single sentence which is external to our
goal in this book. The simple sentence is single when
both its subject and its predicate signify a single idea.
The declarative sentence may also be multiple when
its predicate or its subject or both of them signify several ideas. The combined sentence is single when there
is a link to bring it together, and it is multiple when
there is no link to bring it together. Thus, every sentence is either single or multiple. If it is single, it is
single either because its subject and predicate signify
a single idea, or it is single because of the link bringing
them together. The latter are sentences in which there
is more than one subject and one predicate—for example, conditional and assertional syllogisms. For conditional syllogisms are single due to the link provided
by the conditional particle—like our saying "if the sun
rises, then it is day." For it is the "then" which makes
one sentence out of these two simple sentences—namely,
our saying "the sun rises" and "it is day." Assertional
syllogisms are single due to the link provided by the
middle term—like our saying "man is an animal, and

---

[17] See Aristotle *Rhetoric* I.i.ll.1355ª3-17, I.ii.21-22.1358ª10-35, I.iii.7-
9.1359ª6-26, II.xx.2-xxii.17.1393ª25-1397ª6, and III.xvii.5-9.1418ª1-
21; *Poetics* 1457ª23-30; *Posterior Analytics* II.iii.-xix.90ª35-100ᵇ3.

an animal is a body"—as will be set forth later.[18] If the
sentence is multiple, it is multiple either because its
predicate or its subject or both of them have several
meanings or because they have no link to bring them
together.

17ᵃ11-12   19. Every declarative sentence must have a verb,[19]
or what takes the place of a verb, to link the predicate
with the subject. That is because the declarative sentence, whose subject and predicate are nouns, must
have a verb, or what takes the place of a verb, to signify
the way the predicate is linked to the subject. The verb
is either actually there and is stated, as is the case in
languages other than Arabic, or it is potentially there
and is concealed, as is most often the case in the Arabic
language. For since there are three ideas here—a subject, a predicate, and a connection linking the predicate
to the subject—it is necessary that there be three utterances here—an utterance signifying the subject, an
utterance signifying the predicate, and an utterance
signifying the connection. The utterance signifying the
way the predicate is linked to the subject sometimes
signifies the way it is linked in time past or time to
come or now—like your saying "Zayd is learned now"
or "Zayd was learned" or "Zayd will be learned"—and
sometimes it signifies the way it is linked without time
restriction. The latter is necessary predication, and it
is like someone saying "the angles of the triangle are
equal to two right angles." There is no utterance in
the Arabic language which signifies this type of link,
even though it is found in all the other languages. The
utterance most closely resembling it in the Arabic language is what the word "is"[20] or "exists" signifies, as in

---

[18] See Aristotle *Prior Analytics* I.iv.25ᵇ36-37 and Averroes *Middle
Commentary on Aristotle's Prior Analytics*, ed. C. Butterworth et al. (Cairo:
GEBO, 1982), para. 27.

[19] Averroes adds "I mean a *fi'l.*" See above, para. 9, note 7, and
para. 13, note 13.

[20] The word is *huwa*; according to al-Fārābī, this word was used
by the early Arab philosophers in order to indicate what the Persian

our saying "Zayd is an animal" or in our saying "Zayd exists as an animal."

20. There is no assertion or denial with respect to the noun and the verb.[21] It is the sentence, however, which does assert or deny. The sentence which asserts or denies is called a declarative sentence and a judgment. With the simple judgment, affirmation is like placing one thing upon another and negation is like taking one thing away from another. And the combined sentence is a composite of this. The simple judgment is also described as being an utterance which signifies that something exists or does not exist—either in past time, or in the future, or in the present, or without qualification.

17a18-24

21. Affirmation is a judgment claiming one thing with respect to another, and negation is a judgment disclaiming one thing with respect to another. Now on the basis of what is in the soul, one may make a verbal judgment to the effect that what exists outside the soul does not exist, or that what does not exist outside the soul does exist, or that what does exist exists, or that what does not exist is non-existent. And this may be an unqualified judgment or it may be with reference to one of the three times—namely, the present, the past, or the future. Thus, it is quite possible for anything affirmed by one person to be negated by someone else and for anything negated by one person to be affirmed by someone else. And since this is so, it follows that for every affirmation there is a negation opposed to it and that for every negation there is an affirmation opposed to it. This holds insofar as the negation and affirmation exist within the soul, not outside it. For things affirmed insofar as they do exist

17a25-38

---

hast or the Greek *estin* (i.e., our "is") indicates. See al-Fārābī *Kitāb al-Ḥurūf (The Book of Letters)*, ed. M. Mahdi (Beirut: Imprimerie Catholique, 1969), para. 83.

[21] The terms used here for assertion and denial (*ṣidq* and *kadhb*) are the same terms translated heretofore as truth and falsehood; cf. para. 17.

outside the soul do not admit of an opposing negation, nor do things negated insofar as they do exist outside the soul admit of an opposing affirmation. But the inquiry into affirmation and negation is from the perspective of their being in the soul. A negation and an affirmation are truly opposed when the idea set forth in them as a predicate is a single idea in all respects and when the same holds for the idea set forth as a subject. When they are not single, either because of ambiguity or the rest of the things set down in the *Sophistics*,[22] then they are not affirmations and negations in opposition.

[22] See Aristotle *On Sophistical Refutations* 175ª1-183ª36 with 165ᵇ12-174ᵇ40.

Chapter Two

22. Ideas[1] are of two sorts, either universal or particular—that is, individual. By universal, I mean that
which is such as to be predicated of more than one
entity—like predicating animal of man, horse, and the
rest of the species of animals. By particular, I mean
that which is not such, that is, such as to be predicated
of more than one entity—like Zayd, ʿAmr, and what
is designated. If this is the case, then it follows necessarily that whenever we make an affirmative or negative judgment about something, that judgment must
be about one of the individual ideas or about one of
the universal ideas. Next, if it is about one of the universal ideas, then it will doubtlessly be taken either
without any limitation or with a limitation—and by
limitation, I mean the utterance "every" and "some."
Next, if it is taken with a limitation, it cannot be with
anything but a universal or particular limitation.

23. Opposites with respect to affirmation and negation which have one of the individual ideas for their
subject are called individual opposites—like our saying
"Zayd is free," "Zayd is not free." Opposites whose
subject is a universal idea taken without limitation, that
is, not predicated of a particular[2] universal idea or of
part of it, but predicated without qualification, are called
indeterminate—like our saying "man is white," "man

---

[1] Averroes, perhaps following the lead of the Arabic translation,
uses the term maʿānī to render Aristotle's *pragmata*, but in Chapter
One, para. 2, he uses this term maʿānī in place of the term *athār*,
which the Arabic translator had used to render Aristotle's *pathēmasta*.
As was mentioned above, *Middle Commentary on Aristotle's Categories*,
para. 1, note 2, the term maʿnā (plural, maʿānī) admits of several
different possible translations: idea, notion, thought, meaning, thing,
and signification are but a few.

[2] Literally, "that" (*dhālika*).

is not white." Opposites whose subject is a universal idea taken with a limitation are three-fold: either a universal limitation is attached to each of the two opposites, or a particular limitation is attached to each of them, or a particular limitation is attached to one of them and a universal limitation to the other. Those to both of which a universal limitation is attached are called contrary—like our saying "every man is white" and "not a single man is white." Those to one of which a universal limitation is attached and to the other a particular limitation are called contradictory. These are of two sorts. Either the universal is attached to the affirmation and the particular is attached to the negation—like our saying "every man is white," "not every man is white" or "some people are not white," for the particular negation is expressed in these two ways—or the converse, I mean, the universal limitation is attached to the negation and the particular limitation to the affirmation—like someone saying "a certain man is white" and "not a single man is white." Those having a particular limitation attached to both the affirmation and the negation[3] are called subordinate to the contrary—like our saying "a certain man is white," "a certain man is not white." Thus, there are six sorts of opposites with respect to affirmation and negation: individual; indeterminate; contradictory, which is of two sorts; contrary; and subordinate to the contrary. There is no other division of propositions with respect to the limitation being attached to the predicate, because when the limitation is attached to the predicate, it is either false or superfluous. An example of its falseness is our saying "every man is every animal." And an example of its being superfluous is our saying "every man is some animal" or "every man is every laughing creature."

17ᵇ24-18ᵃ4   24. The sorts of propositions having been settled,

---

[3] Literally, "to each of them" or "to both of them" (*bikull wāḥid minhimā*).

we will say that individual opposites are always divided into truth and falsehood—that is, when one of the two is false, the other is true; and when one of the two is true, the other is false. It is not possible for both of them to be true nor both false—like your saying "Zayd went out," "Zayd did not go out." And upon reflection this is self-evident. Contradictory opposites are also divided into truth and falsehood in all of the moods. With contrary opposites, it is not possible for both of them to be true. But with subordinate contrary opposites, it is possible for both of them to be true. Indeterminate opposites may have a contrary judgment or a subordinate contrary judgment. The reason for this is that the *alif* and the *lām*[4] and what takes their place in other languages signify in one instance the same thing as the universal limitations signify and in another instance the same thing as the particular limitations signify. When they signify what the universal limitations signify, they have the force of the contrary opposites. And when they signify what the particular limitations signify, they have the force of the subordinate contrary opposites. That is because when the *alif* and the *lām* signify the same thing as "some" signifies,[5] they may both be true—as in our saying "man is white," "man is not white." And when the *alif* and the *lām* signify the same thing as the universal limitation signifies, they may both be false.

25. Now these sorts of opposites can exist according 18^a12-17 to the conditions just described—that is, some of them always being divided into truth and falsehood, some being both true, and some being both false—only when attention is paid to taking a single negation for a single affirmation and a single affirmation for a single negation along with the rest of the stipulations that were

---

[4] Or "the"; when combined with a noun, *alif* and *lām* sometimes function as the definite article.

[5] In English, this partitive sense comes about when the article "the" is omitted, whereas in Arabic—as, for example, in French—the article is not so restrictive; see above, para. 23 beginning.

stated. But this is not so when more than one negative
is taken for a single affirmation, as when a universal
and a particular negative are taken for a universal affirmative—like taking "not a single man is white" and
"not every man is white" as the opposite of our saying
"every man is white." Nor is it so when a particular
and a universal affirmative are taken for a universal
negative—like taking "a certain man is white" [and]
"every man is white" as the opposite of our saying "not
a single man is white." Indeed, it is this way because a
single negation is a negation only for a single affirmation, and likewise a single affirmation is an affirmation only for a single negation. An indication of this
is that the negative negates only the predicated idea
which the speaker affirmed to be the predicate of the
very thing he affirmed as its subject, regardless of
whether that subject is one of the individual ideas or
one of the universal ideas and whether a universal or
a particular limitation is attached to it. For if the predicate of the affirmation is different from the predicate
of the negation or if its subject is different from the
subject of the negation, there is another negation for
that affirmation and another affirmation for that negation. The affirmation and the negation are single
when the utterance serving as the predicate and subject
in them signifies a single idea, regardless of whether
the subject is a particular idea or a universal idea and
whether a universal limitation is attached to a universal
idea or not—like in our saying:

every man is white	not every man is white
man is white	man is not white

when we posit "man" and "white" as signifying a single
idea.

18ª18-28   26. When the utterance serving as the subject or the
predicate in pairs of opposites[6] does not signify a single
idea, neither the affirmation nor the negation is single.

---

[6] Literally, "in both of them" or "in the two of them" (*fīhimā*).

For example, when someone posits one name such as
"garment" for both man and horse and says "the garment is white," "the garment is not white," this affirmation is not a single affirmation nor is this negation
a single negation. That is because when we say "the
garment is white," it has the sense of two affirmations.
For it means what our saying "the man is white" and
"the horse is white" means; and these are two propositions, not one. Likewise, our saying "the garment is
not white" has the sense of two negations—namely,
our saying "the horse is not white" and "the man is
not white." It is this way because of the utterance they
have in common, that is, our saying "the garment."
Similarly, the proposition whose predicate, or subject,
or both have a noun in common is not a single proposition but many propositions which are as numerous
as the ideas signified by that common noun. If this is
so, then with the pairs of opposites which are instances
of these propositions having a noun in common—that
is, the contradictory and the individual—there is no
necessity that one be true and the other false. The
discussion of when propositions having subjects or
predicates with many meanings are single and when
they are not will be taken up again.[7]

27. Here, then, are three conditions that ought to
be stipulated with respect to pairs of opposites so that
they are taken as opposites in the manner we have
described. One is that their subject and predicate be
single in all respects, not taken in one respect with one
and in a different respect with the other. The second
is that the affirmation and the negation be single. The
third is that what is set down as the opposite of a single
affirmation be a single negation. From this it has become clear when opposites are opposites, how many
sorts of opposites there are, and what conditions pertain to them.

28. We say: with respect to these pairs of opposites,   18ᵃ29-30

---

[7] See para. 57.

those that are always divided into truth and falsehood in all of the moods are the individual and contradictory ones. With matters existing in the present or the past, they must necessarily be divided into truth and falsehood in that one of the two is in itself true and the other false, regardless of whether we know the true one from the false one or not. Thus, it is clear in itself that one of the two sentences about whether Zayd exists now or not is necessarily true and the other false, regardless of whether we have reached the point of distinguishing between what is true and what is false or not, for its existence is definite in itself. It is the same with past things and with necessary matters whose existence has no time stipulation.

18ᵃ33-34   29. Matters existing in the future—namely, possible things—do not divide into truth and falsehood in a completely definite manner.[8] That is because in this mood these pairs of opposites inevitably fall into divisions. Either they divide into truth and falsehood or they do not. Next, if they do divide into truth and falsehood, they do so either in a definite or an indefinite manner. And if they do not divide into truth and falsehood, then they are either both true, or both false, or both of these states exist in them.

18ᵃ35-18ᵇ5   30. If every affirmation and negation divides into truth and falsehood in a completely definite manner,[9] each thing must be existent or non-existent. And from this it follows that when one man says some future thing will come to be and another man says it will not come to be, one of these two sentences is true and the other false. That is because both of these cannot exist at the same time—I mean, being and non-being. Now the nature of the existent thing follows upon the true sentence, and the true sentence follows upon it. For if a man says that a certain thing is white and what he says is true, there must be white outside the soul; and

---

[8] Literally, "definitely in itself" (*'alā al-taḥṣīl fī nafsih*).
[9] See preceding note.

if what he says is false, there must be non-white outside
the soul. If we say that it is non-white and what we say
is true, there must be non-white outside the soul; if
what we say is false, there must be white outside the
soul. It is the same with the converse of this—namely,
if the thing outside the soul is white, the true sentence
concerning it must be that it is white and the false one
that it is not white. And if there is non-white outside
the soul, then the true sentence about it is that it is not
white and the false one that it is white.

31. If the mutually opposite affirmation and nega-   18ᵇ6-9
tion divide into truth and falsehood with respect to
future matters in that the existence of one of the two
is definite in itself, then future matters exist in a necessary manner and nothing here exists by chance or
due to an indefinite cause. Nor does anything exist of
which it is said that it is possible for it to come into
being and not to come into being; rather, the coming
into being or not coming into being of anything is
necessary. And that follows from truth or[10] falsehood
in itself definitely being in one of the two opposites.
That is because it is not permissible for what is not
true to be brought into existence, either by way of
affirmation or by way of negation. For if that were
permissible, the existence of truth in one of the two
opposites would not be definite in itself. And if the
existence of truth and falsehood in the two opposites
were not definite in itself, the possibility of a thing
coming into being and not coming into being would
be one and the same. Likewise, if the possibility of a
thing coming into being or not coming into being were
one and the same, the existence of truth and falsehood
in the two opposites stating it would not be definite in
itself. Thus affirming something would have no greater
authority than negating it and negating it no greater
authority than affirming it. Nor would it have any greater

---

[10] Literally, "and" (wa).

authority simply because it is affirmed or negated by someone.

18ᵇ10-17   32. From this it follows that if a given thing becomes white at a given moment, to say of it before it becomes white that it will become white is true and necessary. Likewise, with anything coming to be, it is as true to say of it before it comes to be that it will come to be as to say so at the moment it comes to be, and the truth of saying that it exists in the present is thus the same as the truth of saying that it will exist in the future. If this is so, it is not possible for the possible thing—which is not existent now and of which it is said that it will exist—not to exist. And when it is not possible for something not to exist, it is absurd that it not exist. When it is absurd for a thing not to exist, it must exist. And whatever must be, necessarily exists. Therefore all things necessarily exist. If this is so, then there is nothing here which occurs by chance nor anything disposed so as to come into being and not to come into being. That is because what occurs by chance is of this description—I mean, its coming into being is not necessarily requisite—just as anything whose coming into being or not coming into being is necessarily requisite does not occur by chance.

18ᵇ18-25   33. Moreover, it is not permissible for you to say that with respect to future matters the negation and affirmation both hold and are thus both true or that both are eliminated and are thus both false—for instance, that our two statements about something, that it is possible for it to come to be and that it is possible for it not to come to be, are both true or both false. For if they were both false, it would result that the contradictory pair of opposites[11] does not divide into truth and falsehood in all the moods, which is something whose incongruity has already been explained.[12] The

---

[11] "Of opposites" added for clarity; the text has "the two contradictories" (*al-mutanāqiḍān*).

[12] See paras. 24 and 28.

same would result if both were true. What is more, if both were true, it would result that the thing is both existent and non-existent. Not only is that absurd, it also amounts to eliminating the nature of the possible. And if they were false, the result would be that the thing is neither existent nor non-existent.

34. This is the absurdity which results if we claim 18^b26-19^a7
that the opposites which do or do not divide into truth and falsehood definitely in all the moods with respect to future matters are both true or both false. It is evident that many repugnant things result when we eliminate the nature of the possible and maintain that all future matters are necessary. The first is that deliberation and preparation so as to repel an anticipated evil or provision for an attainable good are rendered invalid. So a man's thinking that if he performs a particular act it will lead to a particular consequence and that if he does not do so the consequence will not come about becomes an invalid consideration and an unsound belief. This reaches the point of resulting in the following repugnant thing: if a certain man deliberates about a certain event and pronounces that it will occur in, for example, ten thousand years and sets about preparing the causes requisite for its occurring and coming to be within this long period of time, if a man were to live for so long, and if another man deliberates about how to prevent it occurring in this very same period of time and considers how to prepare the causes which will prevent its occurring, what each of them does is invalid and futile and each one's deliberation is in vain and senseless. That is because whichever one of the two beliefs is in itself true must necessarily come to exist, regardless of whether one of the two men deliberates about how to invalidate it and the other about how to make it exist or neither one deliberates about it. From this it follows that will is not a cause of any given thing occurring, but that all things run their course by nature and according to which of the con-

tradictory pair of opposites[13] pertains to them, even if no human being deliberates about bringing one of those things into existence or about preventing its existence. And the judgment of someone who deliberates about something for ten thousand years is the same as the judgment of someone who deliberates about it for a short time, however short it may be, and even the same as the judgment of someone who does not deliberate about it at all.

19ª8-17   35. All of these things are extremely repugnant and contrary to our natural disposition. That is because we do see things here the principle of whose occurrence is reflection and provision being taken for them. Moreover, with respect to matters that are not actual, some may appear to be so disposed by their nature that a thing and its opposite are brought into being through them without distinction—I mean that it is equally possible for something to be brought into being through them or not. For example, a garment may be torn before it has been worn out or it may not be torn but nonetheless worn out. That is because these two conditions are equally possible for the garment. The same holds for all matters which come to be in this mood with this kind of possibility and potentiality.

19ª18-23   36. If this is so, it is evident that not all things are necessary. It becomes evident instead that things are of two sorts, either necessary or possible, and that possible things are of three sorts. There is the equally possible, in which the existence of something is not more likely than its non-existence nor its non-existence more likely than its existence. There is the probable,[14] in which one of the two opposites is more likely to come into existence than the second and the occurrence of the second is less frequent. Both kinds of the

[13] "Of opposites" added for clarity; the text has "the two contradictories" (*al-mutanāqiḍayn*).

[14] Or "more possible" or even "possible more often than not" (*mumkin ʿalā al-akthar*).

possible exist in this genus—I mean, what is probable[14]
and what is improbable.[15]

37. With respect to necessary things, some are nec-   19ª24-28
essary in an absolute sense. These are the things which
are always existent or which are always non-existent.
And some are not necessary in an absolute sense. These
are the things whose existence is necessary at the moment in which they exist or things whose non-existence
is necessary at the moment in which they are non-
existent. They are of two types. Either they are things
whose predicates necessarily exist for their subjects as
long as their subjects exist—like reason existing for a
certain man when that man exists—or things which are
non-existent as long as their subjects are non-existent.
Or they are things which exist as long as they exist—
like a man existing as long as he exists.

38. If these are the natural divisions of existence and   19ª28-19ᵇ4
if the way the negation and the affirmation are divided
into truth and falsehood must conform to existence
outside the soul, then it is evident that the pairs of
opposites which divide into truth and falsehood in all
the moods divide into truth and falsehood with respect
to the sorts of necessary matters in a completely definite manner—I mean, in such a manner that the true
opposite and the false opposite are completely definite—outside the soul, even if we are not aware of how
things stand and are ignorant of it. Now they also divide into truth and falsehood with respect to future
matters in the possible mood. That is because one of
the two contradictories must exist in the future, yet
not in a completely definite manner, but rather in a
not definite manner, as they are naturally, which is the
way they are for us. Therefore it is not possible to
acquire knowledge of this genus, for the matter is in
itself unknown. But with respect to what is probable[16]
not with respect to what is equally possible, one of the

---

[15] Or "less possible" or even "possible less often than not" (*mumkin*
'alā al-aqall).

[16] Or "more possible"; see para. 36, note 14.

two opposites is more likely to be true than the other, since its existence is more likely than its non-existence. With respect to this genus, it is possible to acquire knowledge about the occurrence of one of them before it occurs—I mean, about the occurrence of the one which is such as to occur more often. Common to every pair of opposites which is such as to divide into truth and falsehood is that it divides into truth and falsehood with respect to future matters in the possible mood, not definitely. But with respect to what is equally possible, neither one of the opposites is more likely to be true than the other. With respect to what is probable,[17] one of the two opposites is more likely to be true than the other. With respect to what is improbable,[18] one of the two opposites is more likely to be false than the other.

39. From this it has become clear how pairs of opposites divide into truth and falsehood with respect to all matters. And that is with respect to those opposites which are such as to divide into truth and falsehood always, namely, the contradictory and the individual opposites.

[17] Or "possible for the most part" (*al-mumkinah al-akthariyah*).
[18] Or "less possible"; see para. 36, note 15.

CHAPTER THREE

40. Now[1] some propositions are binary, namely, those which have a verb as a predicate. And some are ternary, namely, those which have a noun as a predicate. Those which have a verb as a predicate are called binary, because they are made up of a predicate and a subject alone. And those which have a noun as a predicate are called ternary, because they are made up of a subject, a linking verb, and a predicate. Moreover, the noun and the verb which make up the propositions are either definite or indefinite. So it is evident that every binary proposition is made up either of a definite noun and a definite verb—like our sentence "man exists"—of an indefinite noun and an indefinite verb— like our sentence "not-man not-exists"—of a definite noun and an indefinite verb—like our sentence "man not-exists"—or of an indefinite noun and a definite verb—like our sentence "not-man exists." However, it is not customary to use the indefinite verb in these kinds of propositions—I mean, binary ones. That is because in these the position of the particle of negation is not distinguished from that of the particle of retraction, since the position of the particle of negation is the same as that of the particle of retraction. Therefore, in the languages that use the retractive, no binary proposition in which the verb is retractive is found. Therefore, two of these four sorts of propositions are omitted—the sort in which both the predicate and the subject are indefinite and the sort in which the pred-

---

[1] This is the beginning of a long conditional sentence whose apodosis is the phrase "so it is evident . . . 'not-man exists.' " The idea is that *since* there are two kinds of propositions whose subject and predicate may be definite or indefinite, *then* they can evidently be structured in four different ways.

icate is indefinite—and two sorts remain. So with respect to these propositions, there are two pairs of opposites and four premises. If we multiply these two
pairs of opposites by the six preceding pairs of opposites,[2] there will be twelve pairs of opposing binary
propositions and twenty-four propositions. And because the verb in every one of the binary propositions
either signifies present time, future time, or past time,
if we multiply these three by the twenty-four propositions, there will be seventy-two propositions in this
genus and thirty-six pairs of opposites. And if we multiply them by the three moods—namely, the possible,
the necessary, and the impossible—the total number
of propositions will be two hundred and sixteen.

19ᵇ20-26   41. There are twice as many ternary propositions as
binary propositions and twice as many pairs of ternary
opposites. That is because the four sorts of opposites
are feasible in them: I mean, the sort in which the
subject and the predicate noun are definite, and these
are known as simple, like our saying "man is just,"
"man is not just"; the sort in which both nouns are
indefinite, like our saying "not-man is not-just," "not-
man is not not-just"; and the two remaining sorts—I
mean, those which have one definite and one indefinite
noun, either the predicate or the subject—and their
opposites.

42. If ternary propositions which have a definite noun
as a subject and either a definite or an indefinite noun
as a predicate are placed in a four-sided figure along
with their opposites, the opposites being on the two
horizontal sides and the non-opposites on the two vertical sides, so that the affirmative of the simple proposition is with the negative of the retractive proposition
on one side and the negative of the simple proposition
is with the affirmative of the retractive proposition on
one side as well, the way the retractive and the simple
propositions imply each other will be the same as the

[2] See para. 23.

way the privative and the simple propositions imply each other.[3] Yet the case of privative with respect to retractive propositions is not the same as that of retractive with respect to simple propositions, and this holds for all six sorts of opposites. By privative propositions, I mean here propositions whose predicate noun signifies either the privation which has already been generally described[4]—like our saying "man is ignorant"—or the more specific[5] of two contraries—like our sentence "man is unjust." With respect to that, let us first look into indeterminate propositions and place them in a four-sided figure as we have stipulated and also place the privative propositions under the retractive propositions in the same way that we placed the retractive propositions under the simple propositions. We will do that by adding to the four-sided figure another figure which will have one of its sides in common with the first figure. For example, we will set down[6] one figure ABCD and set down[6] a figure CDEF joined to it. On the side AB, we will place the affirmative simple proposition and its opposite—namely, "man is just," "man is not just." On the side CD, we will place the negative retractive proposition and its opposite— namely, "man is not not-just," "man is not-just." On the side EF, we will place the negative privative proposition and its opposite—namely, "man is not unjust," "man is unjust." So if you consider these propositions set down in this fashion:

man is just	A	B	man is not just
man is not not-just	C	D	man is not-just
man is not unjust	E	F	man is unjust

---

[3] The figure described by Averroes must be like this:

| man is just | man is not just |
| man is not not-just | man is not-just |

[4] See above, *Middle Commentary on Aristotle's Categories*, paras. 92-93.

[5] Or "more particularly characteristic" (*akhaṣṣ*).

[6] Or "we will place" (*naḍaʿ*).

you will find that those which are on the horizontal lines do not imply each other, for they are opposites. And in what has preceded, you have already been apprised of how they function as opposites.[7]

43. If you consider those which are on the vertical, you will find that the negative retractive proposition is implied by the affirmative simple proposition with respect to truth, but not the converse. That is because if our sentence "man is just" is true, our sentence "man is not not-just" is true. But if our sentence "man is not not-just" is true, it does not result that our sentence "man is just" will be true. For our sentence "man is not not-just" is true of the just man, of the man to whom neither justice nor injustice is attributed—that is, the youngster—and of the man who is not a citizen. Therefore the negative retractive proposition is more generally true[8] than the affirmative simple proposition, since it is true of[9] three situations and the affirmative simple proposition of one. When the general exists, the particular does not exist as a consequence— the way the general exists as a consequence of the particular existing. An example of that is animal and man, for when man exists, animal exists; but when animal exists, man does not exist as a consequence.

44. The converse holds for the negative simple proposition and the affirmative retractive proposition with respect to truth; I mean, the negative simple proposition is implied by the affirmative retractive proposition, not the converse. That is because the negative simple proposition is more generally true[10] than the affirmative retractive proposition, since our sentence "man is not just" is true of[11] the unjust man, the man who is neither unjust nor just—namely, the non-citizen—and the child. And our sentence "man is not-

---

[7] See para. 23.
[8] Or "applies more generally" (*a'amm ṣidqan*).
[9] Or "applies to" (*taṣduq 'alā*).
[10] See para. 43, note 8.
[11] See para. 43, note 9.

just" is only true of[11] the unjust man, for our saying "not-just" signifies privation, and privation—as it was previously defined—is the elimination of something from that in which it is its wont to exist at the moment in which it is its wont to exist in that thing.[12] Thus the affirmative retractive proposition is true of[13] one situation and the negative simple proposition of three.

45. When the way they imply each other with respect to falsehood is looked into, it will be the converse of this; I mean, the affirmative simple proposition is implied by the negative retractive proposition. That is because the negative retractive proposition is false in a more specific[14] manner than the affirmative simple proposition. For our sentence "man is just" is false with respect to the unjust man and the man who is neither just nor unjust, and our sentence "man is not not-just" is false only with respect to the unjust man. Similarly, the situation concerning the way the negative simple proposition and the affirmative retractive proposition imply each other with respect to falsehood is the converse of the way they imply each other with respect to truth; I mean, the one which implies becomes the one which is implied.

46. When the privative and simple propositions are considered with respect to the way they imply each other, their situation concerning truth and falsehood will be found to be the same as with the retractive and simple propositions. Those which are on the diagonal—namely, the diagonal AD—are contraries from the aspect of the moods. Their situation will be made known in what follows.[15]

47. If the other sorts of opposites—I mean, the contradictory, the individual, the contrary, and the subordinate contrary propositions—are set down in this   19ᵇ31-32

---

[12] See above, *Middle Commentary on Aristotle's Categories*, paras. 92-93.

[13] See para. 43, note 9.

[14] Or "more particularly characteristic" (*akhaṣṣ*).

[15] See para. 47 and paras. 72-83.

fashion, they will be found to imply each other in a single way. But the situation differs with respect to each sort that is on the diagonal. That is because with some both can be true, and with others both can be false. With respect to these, Aristotle only mentioned what we have mentioned and he deferred the issue until the *Prior Analytics*.[16] The general rule for knowing the way these imply each other is that whenever two of these premises agree with respect to quantity—namely, the limitation—and differ with respect to quality—namely, negation and affirmation as well as retraction and non-retraction—they imply each other. I mean, the more general is implied by the more particular.[17] Those which do not imply each other are opposites in the manner of contraries or contradictories, as has been said.[18]

19ᵇ33-20ᵃ3   48. When an indefinite noun is taken as the subject of ternary propositions and a definite noun is taken as a predicate of them at one time and an indefinite noun at another, there will occur in this genus affirmative and negative simple and retractive propositions other than those which have been set forth. The simple ones will be those which have a definite noun as a predicate—as with the first sort of simple propositions—and the retractive ones those which have an indefinite noun as a predicate. That is because it is with regard to its predicate, not its subject, that a proposition is interpreted as being simple or retractive. The affirmative simple proposition in this genus will be like our sentence "not-man is just," and its negative will be "not-man is not just." The affirmative retractive proposition will be our sentence "not-man is not-just," and its negative will be "not-man is not not-just." It is clear that these two pairs of opposites occurring in this genus of

---

[16] See Aristotle *Prior Analytics* II.xv.63ᵇ31-64ᵇ27 and Averroes *Middle Commentary on Aristotle's Prior Analytics*, paras. 337-342.

[17] That is, in the same way as things which exist by nature imply each other; see above, para. 43, and also below, para. 81.

[18] See above, paras. 42 and 46.

ternary propositions—I mean, those which have an indefinite noun as a subject—are different from the two pairs of opposites occurring in the sort of propositions which have a definite noun as a subject, for the subject of these is a privation of the subject of those. The sorts of privation signified by the indefinite noun have been commented upon elsewhere.[19]

49. If negatives are made of this sort of propositions, the particle of negation does not take the place of the particle of retraction, nor does one of the two compensate for the other. Instead, the particle of negation should be given a distinct place in them. For those which have limitations, it goes with the limitation—as is the case with the first sort of ternary propositions. For indeterminate and individual propositions, it goes with the existential verb. The particle of retraction is always placed with the subject so that for the negative simple propositions belonging to this genus it, along with the particle of negation, will be brought forward twice—in propositions having a limitation, with the limitation as well as with the subject; and in indeterminate and individual propositions, with the existential verb as well as with the subject. For retractive propositions, it is brought forward three times—once with the limitation or existential verb, a second time with the subject, and a third time with the predicate. One of the two particles of negation in these propositions does not compensate for the other—I mean, the particle of retraction does not really take the place of the particle of negation—even though both are negations. The particle of retraction makes no assertion or denial[20] when it is attached to the subject, whereas the particle of negation does make an assertion or a denial[21] when it is attached to the subject. For example, the negation of our sentence "every not-man is just" is our sentence

---

[19] See above, *Middle Commentary on Aristotle's Categories*, paras. 92-93; also here, paras. 10, 23, 24, and 57.

[20] Literally, "is neither true nor false" (*lais yaṣduq wa lā yakdhib*).

[21] Literally, "is either true or false" (*ṣadaq aw kadhab*).

"not every not-man is just," not our sentence "not every man is just." And the negation of our sentence "every not-man is not-just" is our sentence "not every not-man is not-just." That comes about through our bringing the particle of negation forward in three places, not by our bringing it forward in two places, as when we say "not every man is not-just."[22]

20ª4-23   50. The case is the same with the binary propositions in this genus—I mean, the simple ones, for we have already said that according to the signs of the commonly known languages there are no retractive propositions among them.[23] With these, the particle of negation should also be given a place twice—once with the subject and once with the limitation in propositions having a limitation, or with the verb itself[24] in individual and indeterminate propositions. Here, too, it is not enough to have one without the other. For example, just as the negation of our sentence "every man walks"— which is a proposition having a definite noun as a subject—is our sentence "not every man walks," so, too, the negation of our sentence "every not-man walks" is our sentence "not every not-man walks," not our sentence "not every man walks" nor "not every man not-walks." For the particle of negation does not take the place of the particle of retraction nor does the particle of retraction take its place, since each of them eliminates from the proposition something other than what the other eliminates. That is because the particle of negation in propositions having limitations only eliminates the universal judgment contained in the universal limitation or the particular judgment contained

---

[22] Although Averroes does use the term "particle of negation" (*ḥarf al-salb*) here to comprehend both the particle of negation and the particle of retraction (*ḥarf al-ʿadl*), he seems to do so because both are negations—as stated earlier—and not because he considers them to be interchangeable.

[23] See para. 40.

[24] According to the explanation of the preceding paragraph as well as of paras. 12 and 40, this verb would be an existential verb.

in the particular limitation, whereas the particle of retraction only eliminates the universal subject or the
universal predicate, not the universal judgment. That
is because the universal limitation attached to the proposition does not signify that the posited idea is universal
in such a way that its elimination would result in the
posited universal idea being eliminated. Instead, it only
signifies that the judgment about the universal idea is
universal. This is clear with indeterminate statements,
for it does not follow from their not having limitations
that the ideas posited in them are not universal, if the
utterances in them have universal significance—like
our sentence "man is just," "man is not just." For the
utterance "man" signifies a universal idea, even if the
utterance "every" is not attached to it. If the utterance
"every" were what signified that the idea is universal,
the utterance "man" would not signify a universal idea
unless "every" were attached to it. That is why in propositions having limitations whose subjects are indefinite
nouns—whether they mutually imply or oppose each
other—the particle of negation must be attached to the
limitation and be repeated a second time with the subject. If they are retractive, it is repeated a third time
with the predicate. If they are not retractive, it is enough
to repeat it with the subject. In the possible mood,
instances may arise when the particle of retraction has
the same force as the particle of negation for dividing
into truth and falsehood in all the moods. And in some
instances that is not the consequence.

51. The instance in which the particle of retraction
has the same force as the particle of negation is when
the subjects of individual propositions are taken as existing at the moment in which they are such as to have
a state or the privation opposed to it as an attribute.
For example, when a questioner asks with respect to
Socrates "is he just or not just" and the true answer is
"he is not just," but instead of answering the questioner
by saying "he is not just," it is said "he is not-just." For
the force of our saying "not-just" here would be the

20ª23-26

same as our saying "not just" if our sentence were "Socrates is just or not-just" and there happened to exist in it the two preceding stipulations which divide into truth and falsehood in the same way our sentence "Socrates is just or not just" divides into them.

52. As the commentators say, if in this instance the questioner had intended to get the answerer to admit to an affirmative premise but received a negative one as a reply, he may take a retractive premise instead of the negative one. Then he could make use of it for the syllogism by putting it in the spot in which the affirmative premise, but not the negative one, is used—as with the minor premise in the first figure. For—as will be explained in the *Prior Analytics*—when the minor premise in the first figure is negative, it cannot be used to bring about a conclusion.[25] The questioner can also use this piece of advice if he wants to conclude something contradictory from the negative. However, the interpretation we have given is more appropriate for the purpose of this book.

20ª26-31   53. The instance in which the particle of retraction, though joined with the state, does not have the force of the particle of negation for dividing into truth and falsehood is with respect to universal propositions in this mood—as when the questioner asks "is every man wise or is every man not wise" and instead of saying "every man is not wise," the answerer replies with "every man is not-wise." That is because for our sentence "every man is wise," the opposite which always divides into truth and falsehood is our sentence "every man is not wise," not our sentence "every man is not-wise." For our saying "wise" and "not-wise" has the force of contraries—namely, our saying "every man is wise" and "not a single man is wise." And as was previously explained, contraries may both be false in this mood.[26]

20ª32-37   54. The opposition between the definite and indef-

[25] See Averroes *Middle Commentary on Aristotle's Prior Analytics*, paras. 33, 41, and 43.
[26] See above, para. 47.

inite noun and between the definite and indefinite verb
is not of the same genus as the opposition between the
affirmation and the negation. For in the languages in
which nouns like these are used, our saying "not-man"
does not signify what our saying "not man" signifies.
Our saying "not man" signifies a subject of which humanity has been negated, even if it is not made explicit
in this saying. Therefore it is a compound sentence.
Our saying "not healthy" has a similar meaning. When
we say "not-man" and "not-healthy" without attaching
a noun or verb to them explicitly, they do not signify
what the negation does. Instead, our saying "not-man"
only signifies the privation of humanity and our saying
"not-healthy" the privation of health—and this is the
uncombined idea that our saying "sickness" signifies.
It becomes evident that they do not have the same
significance as the negation due to the fact that the
negation is true or false, whereas our saying "not-man"
is neither true nor false. That is because if our saying
"man" is neither true nor false as long as no informing
verb[27] is attached to it, even though it does signify a
state and an existent form, then it is more likely that
our saying "not-man" will not signify truth or falsehood since it signifies not a definite being, but only an
indefinite being.

55. Simple and retractive propositions which have   20ᵃ37-40
an indefinite noun as a subject imply each other, as is
the case with simple and retractive propositions which
have a definite noun as a subject. That is because our
sentence "every not-man is not-just"—which is an affirmative retractive proposition in this genus—signifies
the same thing as our sentence "anything which is not-
man is not just"—which is a negative simple proposition. Between this sort of proposition—I mean, the one
whose subject is an indefinite noun—and the sort of

[27] That is, as long as no verb which says that man is doing something is attached to it. The term is *khabar*; see above, paras. 9 and
12.

proposition whose subject is a definite noun, there is neither mutual implication nor opposition.

20ᵇ1-13   56. When the order of the predicate noun, the subject, or the linking verb in ternary propositions or the order of the subject or predicate—I mean, the verb—in binary propositions is altered, the statement itself nonetheless remains one. It preserves its truth if it is true or its falsehood if it is false. Instances of this alteration are setting at the beginning what is such as to come last, or bringing forth first what is such as to be brought forth second, or bringing forth later what is such as to be brought forth earlier, and in general changing their order while keeping the predicate a predicate and the subject a subject.[28] An example of that is our saying "man is just," "just is man." For this proposition is one and the same, as is our saying "Zayd arose," "arose Zayd."[29] If propositions which differ only with respect to the way their parts are ordered in terms of being prior or subsequent were not the same, the consequence would be that there would be more than one negative for a single proposition. And it has already been explained that a single affirmative has only a single negative.[30] That is because if our sentence "man is just" and our sentence "just is man" were not a single proposition but were two propositions differing in meaning, and if the negation of our sentence "man is just" were our sentence "man is not just" and the negation of our sentence "just is man" were "not just is man," and if it were also clear that our sentence "not just is man" were a negation of our sentence "man is just," the consequence would be that for our sentence "man is just" there would be two negations. One would be our sentence "man is not just," and the other would

---

[28] This sentence and the two preceding ones form one long sentence in the Arabic text.

[29] Though it is not correct to say "arose Zayd" in English, it is as correct to say *qām Zayd* (arose Zayd) in Arabic as to say *Zayd qām* (Zayd arose).

[30] See para. 25.

be "not just is man"—that is, the negation of the proposition we posited as changing the meaning of our
sentence "man is just," namely, our sentence "just is
man." Now, that these two negations are one is more
readily known than that these two affirmatives are one.
Thus it has become clear that when the nouns and
verbs which are parts of propositions are given an order in speech other than the usual and current one in
that language—I mean, other than the order which is
most eloquent—and the predicate remains a predicate
and the subject a subject, the proposition remains itself.

57. When a single noun is affirmed of several nouns   20ᵇ14-22
or several nouns are affirmed of a single noun or when
a single noun is negated of several nouns or several
nouns are negated of a single noun, then that affirmation is not single nor is that negation single—just
as when a single noun is affirmed or negated of a single
noun, there is no single affirmation or negation as long
as the idea signified by that single word is not single,
as was said in what has preceded—unless those several
nouns signify a single idea.[31] That occurs either by
those several nouns being synonymous[32]—which is when
each one signifies the same idea—or by those several
nouns signifying parts of a definition or general description of a single thing—like our saying "man is an
animal" and "man is rational," for bringing these two
predicates together constitutes the definition of man,
which is that man is a rational animal. The same holds
as well if a general description of him is given—like
our saying "man is an animal" and "man is two-legged"—
for the composite is a general description of man,
namely, that he is a two-legged animal. The utterance
"man" signifies in a summary manner the same thing
each of these sentences signifies separately. If bringing
the several predicates together does not constitute a

---

[31] See paras. 26-27.

[32] See above, *Middle Commentary on Aristotle's Categories*, para. 4; the
term used here is *asmā mutarādifah*, whereas the term used there is
asmā mutawāṭi'ah.

single thing, then the affirmation based on them is not single nor is the negation based on them single. Similarly, if a single predicate is predicated of several subjects, that constitutes neither a single affirmation nor a single negation. An example of that is our predicating of man that he is "white" and that he is "walking," for if these two were predicated of man together and it were said "man is white, walking," that would not signify a single idea except by accident. And this case is the same as the one where an ambiguous[33] utterance signifying more than a single idea is taken as a predicate and predicated of a single subject or where an ambiguous[33] utterance is taken as a subject and a single predicate signifying a single idea is predicated of it. I mean, just as the proposition whose predicate is an ambiguous[33] utterance is not a single utterance nor the proposition whose subject is of this description a single proposition, so, too, is the case with the proposition in which several ideas are affirmed of a single subject by means of distinct nouns or with the proposition in which a single predicate is affirmed of several subjects which are signified by means of distinct nouns, as long as bringing these several predicates or subjects together does not constitute a single idea.

20ᵇ23-26   58. When there are several propositions which have an ambiguous[34] noun as a predicate or subject, the dialectical question about them ought not to be a single question nor the dialectical answer a single answer. And this holds whether the single predicate is true of all of the ideas which the ambiguous[34] subject noun signifies, whether all of the ideas signified by the ambiguous[34] predicate noun are true of the single subject, or whether the predicate and subject utterances both signify several ideas, unless all of the ideas signified by the predicate utterance are true of all of the

---

[33] Literally, "shared" (*mushtarak*); see above, *Middle Commentary on Aristotle's Categories*, para. 3, where this term is used as an equivalent of homonym (*ism muttafiq*).

[34] See preceding note.

ideas signified by the subject utterance—as is explained
in the *Topics*.[35] It is not incumbent upon someone answering in a dialectical manner to improve the questioner's question by making him understand the ideas
of which that ambiguous[36] noun is said. For the answerer and the questioner are at the same level of
knowledge with respect to the thing they are arguing
with each other about. And someone questioning in a
dialectical manner aims only at getting the answerer
to admit to one of the two parts of the contradiction
which he wants to set down as a premise to destroy the
answerer's position. So, in dialectic, when the questioner asks the answerer about a premise having an
ambiguous[36] utterance and the answerer admits to one
of the two parts of the contradiction and from one of
these ideas the questioner sets down a premise from
which he seeks as a conclusion the refutation of the
answerer at which he is aiming, it is then up to the
answerer to say "I did not admit this idea; indeed, the
one I admitted was such and such." And then the questioner reaps no benefit from the answerer admitting
to one of the two parts of the contradiction.

59. Questioning in an instructive manner may pro-   20ᵇ27-30
ceed by means of the ambiguous[37] noun, because it is
incumbent upon the teacher to improve the question
by setting out in detail what that ambiguous[37] noun
signifies. Therefore, this question is not a dialectical
question, because this kind of question may require a
detailed account of what the ambiguous[37] noun signifies—like a questioner asking "what is a source" and
the one who answers him saying "it has various meanings—a bodily organ, a well, a sunspot, and other
things."[38] Since with dialectical questions the ques-

[35] See Averroes *Middle Commentary on Aristotle's Topics*, ed. C. Butterworth and A. Haridi (Cairo: GEBO, 1979), para. 335.
[36] See above, para. 57, note 33.
[37] See preceding note.
[38] The Arabic word for "source" (*ʿayn*), that is, well or spring, is
also the word for eye and sunspot.

tioner only asks about one of the two parts of the contradiction so that one of the two will be admitted to him—like asking "is this like this or not like this"—the question ought to be defined so that the answer which applies to it will be defined. And that occurs only if the question is about a synonymous noun.[39]

60. The several predicates which are predicated of a single subject are of four types. Either they are predicates which are true both when uncombined and when brought together and which constitute a single predicate when brought together, and we said that these being brought together constitutes a single proposition.[40] Or they are predicates which are true both when uncombined and when brought together, but whose being brought together does not constitute a single predicate except by accident. Or they are predicates which are true when uncombined and which lead to ridiculous and superfluous speech when brought together. Or they are predicates which are true when uncombined and false when brought together. Because of all this, after we explain that it does not follow that what is true when uncombined is true when brought together without falsehood and superfluity being included in it, we ought to give the rule by which some of these predicates can be distinguished from others.

20ᵇ31-21ᵃ8   61. Thus we say: all of the predicates which are true when alone are not inevitably true when brought together without speech being ridiculous and superfluous. That is clear from the perspective of material examples and from the kind of repugnant consequence attaching to this position if we admit it. From the perspective of material examples, it may be true of Zayd that he is a doctor and that he is discerning—that is, skillful—without the two matters together being inevitably true of him so that we would say of him that he is a discerning doctor. One of the repugnant things

[39] See above, para. 57, note 32.
[40] See above, para. 57.

attaching to someone who says that everything which is true when alone is true when brought together without ridicule attaching to the sentence is that if our saying of Zayd that he is a "man" is true and that he is "white" is true, then saying both of them together must be true—I mean, that Zayd is a "white man." And if we also predicate of him that he is "a white man" and that he is "white" in such a manner that both are uncombined predicates, it follows that it will be true of him that he is "a white, white man." Similarly, if we take this sentence as a single, uncombined predicate and take the first sentence as an uncombined predicate, it will be true of him that he is "a white man, a white, white man" without there being anything ridiculous or superfluous in the speech, even if the matter goes on endlessly, and that is repugnant. Moreover, if several uncombined things were predicated of him, all of the combinations occurring from those uncombined things would inevitably be true of him—I mean, if some were combined with others—and these are endless. So endless things would be true of one subject—such as that if it were true of him that he is "a man" and that he is "white" and that he is "walking," it would follow that it would be true of him that he is "a white, walking man" and that he is "a white, walking man man" and that he is "a white, walking man man man," and similarly that he is "white white" and "walking walking." So the true predicates about him would be endless. From this it has become clear that not everything which is true when taken alone is true when brought together, as many of the ancients used to think.

62. Since this has been explained, let us consider when a single proposition comes about from several ideas being predicated of one idea and from one idea being predicated of several ideas—which occurs when these several ideas being brought together constitutes a true and single idea—and when not. Thus we say: when these several ideas are not accidentally predicated of the subject and one of them is not included 21^a9-19

in another nor encompassed by it—I mean, to the point
that the stipulation be encompassed by the thing possessing the stipulation, the most worthy example of
which being the instance where the stipulation itself is
the thing possessing the stipulation, like our saying
"white Zayd is white," but not by way of emphasis—
then the composite of those ideas is a single idea. When
they are accidentally predicated—like our saying of
Zayd that he is "white" and that he is "walking"—the
composite is not a single idea. The same holds when
the second is contained in the first, because speech is
then superfluous—like our saying of Zayd "he is a living man" in the sense of qualifying "man" by "living,"
for the utterance "man" already includes "living" and
our qualifying it by "living" is therefore ridiculous, as
opposed to qualifying the genus by the differentia.
When the uncombined predicates are divested of these
two attributes—I mean, accidental predication and one
of them being encompassed by another—the proposition is single—like our saying of man that he is "an
animal" and that he is "two-legged."

21ª19-33   63. Of the things which are true when some qualified
by others are taken together as a predicate of a certain
thing, some are true when taken uncombined and some
are not. The ones that are true are those in which two
things come together. One is that the thing which is
stipulated in the sentence encompass nothing opposed
to what is stipulated about it and qualifies it, not by
any one of the four types of opposition[41] that may
happen to arise, whether that opposition be evident
from what the noun signifies—like our saying "a dead
animal," for "dead" is the contrary of "animal" according to the significance of this noun, I mean, the
noun "animal"—or whether it be evident not from what
the noun signifies but from what the definition or general description signifies—like our saying "a dead man,"
for it is evident that "man" is the opposite of "dead"

---

[41] See above, *Middle Commentary on Aristotle's Categories*, para. 89.

from his definition, in which it is said that he is "a rational animal." So when opposition is encompassed in qualifications like these, they are false when they are taken uncombined. For it is true of the dead one that he is a dead man and not true of him that he is a man. The second stipulation is that the qualification not be predicated of the subject accidentally—namely, for the sake of something else—but essentially—namely, for its own sake. For when it is predicated accidentally in this manner, it is false when taken uncombined— like our saying "Imru' al-Qais is a poet" or "is imagined." For if this is taken uncombined and it is said "Imru' al-Qais is,"[42] it is false since he is now non-existent. The reason for that is that the utterance "is" in our sentence is predicated of Imru' al-Qais with respect to him being imagined or a poet, not as a primary predicate for its own sake, that is, without qualification. And our saying of him that he "is" with respect to him being imagined in the mind is a true sentence. Therefore when the utterance "is" is taken in this respect, it is possible for it to be true of the non-existent. And so too, when the utterance "is not" is predicated of something for the sake of something else, it is true of the existent thing and not true of it when it is predicated of it for its own sake—like our saying of a designated Zayd "he is not a weaver," for it is not true of him that he simply is not, just as it is not true of the non-existent that it simply is. Therefore, when the opposite of the qualified thing is not encompassed in the stipulation nor in the qualification, when the qualified thing is signified by its definition or name, and it is not predicated for the sake of something else, then when things like these are taken uncombined as predicates, they must be true when alone just as they are true when brought together.

[42] Or "is existent" (mawjūd). See above, para. 9, note 8. Imru' al-Qais was a very famous pre-Islamic poet who died about 540, supposedly from a poisoned robe which the emperor Justinian sent to him.

CHAPTER FOUR

64. Some[1] propositions have modal inflections and some do not have modal inflections, the modal inflection being the utterance which signifies how the predicate exists with respect to the subject[2]—like our saying "it is necessary that man be an animal" or "it is possible that he be a philosopher." There are two genera of modal inflective utterances. One is the necessary and what follows it with respect to implication and is counted with it—namely, the requisite and the impossible. The latter is also one of the two divisions of the necessary, since what is necessary must either necessarily exist or necessarily not exist—which is the impossible. The second is the possible and what follows it with respect to implication and is counted with it—like our saying "contingent." Because of this we ought to look into what pairs of opposites there are in this genus, as well as into the propositions which mutually imply each other here, both the retractive and the simple ones. The modal inflective utterances are two-fold only because they are intended to signify what conforms to existence, and there are two classes of existence—either potential or actual. "Necessary" is said of what is actual, and "possible" is said of what is potential. So let us first look into the pairs of opposites and then into the propositions which mutually imply each other.

21ª38-21ᵇ6 65. Thus we say: according to unexamined opinion it seems that in propositions like these the particle of negation ought to be placed with the existential utterance which is the link, not with the predicate, as is the

[1] This is the beginning of a long conditional sentence whose apodosis is the clause "because of this . . . simple ones."

[2] Literally, "the quality of the existence of the predicate for the subject" (*kaifiyah wujūd al-maḥmūl li al-mawḍūʿ*).

case with propositions not having modal inflections. That is, the negation of our sentence "man is just" is our sentence "man is not just," not our sentence "man is not-just." That is, since affirmation and negation divide truth and falsehood about all things, if we set down as the negative of our sentence "man is just" our sentence "man is not-just," it follows that with respect to these two sentences, for example, truth and falsehood about all things would be so divided that if it were false for us to say of a piece of wood, for example, "it is a just man," it would be true to say of it that "it is a not-just man."

66. Since the particle of negation is placed with the   21ᵇ7-23
existential verb in ternary or binary propositions, it is supposed that the case is the same with propositions having modal inflections. Accordingly, the negation of our saying of something "it is possible that it is" would be our saying "it is possible that it is not."³ However, it seems that it is true to say of one and the same thing that "it is possible that it is" and "it is possible that it is not." For example, whatever can possibly be cut up can possibly not be cut up and whatever can possibly walk can possibly not walk. That is because the possible is what does not exist necessarily. Therefore it is possible for it to be and not to be. Since it is not possible for two opposites both to be true of one thing, it is clear that the negation of our sentence "it is possible that it is" is not our sentence "it is possible that it is not."

67. Since it has become clear that the particle of   21ᵇ24-32
negation in these propositions—I mean, those having modal inflections—ought to be placed neither with the predicate nor with the existential verb, then it follows that it is to be placed with the modal inflection. Thus

³ This is actually a retractive construction and could therefore also be translated as "it is possible that it not-is." However, such a translation would be very awkward in English and since the Arabic phrase makes as good sense in Arabic as this formulation does in English, it seems preferable to translate it in this more usual manner.

the negation of our saying of something "it is possible that it is" will be our saying "it is not possible that it is." The matter is the same with all the modal inflections we have enumerated, and that follows necessarily. For just as with propositions having no modal inflections we linked the particle of negation to the thing which in predication took the place of the form—namely, the existential verb—not with the thing which took the place of the matter—namely, the predicate—so, here, the particle of negation is placed with the thing which takes the place the existential verb has with respect to predication in propositions having no modal inflections—namely, the modal inflection. That is, since in propositions having no modal inflection the existential verb indicates what kind of condition the predicate has with respect to the subject,[4] the relation[5] of the existential verb to the predicate in these propositions becomes the relation of form to matter. And since this is the same as the relation of the modal inflection to the existential verb—because it indicates how the predicate exists with respect to the subject[6]—its relation to the existential verb is also that of form to matter. Now since the two relations are one and the particle of negation is placed with the verb there, it must be placed with the modal inflection here.

21ᵇ33-22ᵃ9   68. In general, it is self-evident that the negation of our sentence "it is possible that he is" is our sentence "it is not possible that he is," since these two always divide into truth and falsehood. Our saying "it is possible that he is" and "that he is not"[7] are not contradictory propositions, but propositions which mutually imply each other. Similarly, the negation of our sentence "it is possible that he is not"—which is a retractive

----

⁴ Literally, "the quality of the condition of the predicate with respect to the subject" (*kaifiyah ḥāl al-maḥmūl min al-mawḍūʿ*).
⁵ Here and in the rest of this paragraph, the word translated as "relation" is *nisbah*; it has previously been translated as "connection."
⁶ See above, para. 64, note 2.
⁷ See above, para. 66, note 3.

possible proposition—is our sentence "it is not possible that he is not." The negation of our sentence "it is necessary that he is" is our sentence "it is not necessary that he is." And the negation of our sentence "it is necessary that he is not"—which is a retractive necessary proposition—is our sentence "it is not necessary that he is not." Similarly, the negation of our sentence "it is impossible that he is" is our sentence "it is not impossible that he is." And the negation of our sentence "it is impossible that he is not"[8] is our sentence "it is not impossible that he is not." So these are the opposite propositions in this genus.

69. The propositions which mutually imply one another are as I say: the affirmative simple possible proposition—namely, our sentence "it is possible that he is"—has two propositions as implications, the negative impossible—like our sentence "it is not impossible that he is"—and the negative of the necessary—namely, our sentence "it is not necessary that he is." The affirmative retractive possible proposition—like our sentence "it is possible that he is not"—has, according to what is most generally accepted and most known, two propositions as implications. One of the two is the negative of the retractive necessary proposition—namely, our sentence "it is not necessary that he is not." And the second is the negative of the retractive impossible proposition—namely, our sentence "it is not impossible that he is not." The negative of the simple possible proposition—namely, our sentence "it is not possible that he is"—also has two propositions as implications. One of the two is the affirmative of the retractive necessary proposition—namely, our sentence "it is necessary that he is not." And the second is the affirmative of the simple impossible proposition—namely, our sentence "it is impossible that he is." The negative of the retractive possible proposition—like our sentence "it is

22[a]14-23

[8] As is clear from the explanations of the other sentences here, this is a retractive impossible sentence; see also above, para. 66, note 3.

not possible that he is not"—has two propositions as implications. One of the two is the affirmative of the simple necessary proposition—namely, our sentence "it is necessary that he is." And the second is the affirmative of the retractive impossible proposition—namely, our sentence "it is impossible that he is not."

22ª24-32   70. Let us place the pairs of opposites on a horizontal line and the propositions which mutually imply each other under one another. So that will come forth according to this diagram:[9]

it is possible that he is	it is not possible that he is
it is not necessary that he is	it is necessary that he is not
it is not impossible that he is	it is impossible that he is
it is possible that he is not	it is not possible that he is not
it is not necessary that he is not	it is necessary that he is
it is not impossible that he is not	it is impossible that he is not

22ª33-37   71. If we consider this generally accepted line of implication and follow it out, we will find that our saying "it is impossible" and our saying "it is not impossible" are implied by our saying "it is possible" and

---

[9] What follows is the way the diagram appears in all of the manuscripts. However, Averroes' argument can be more easily grasped if the diagram is arranged, according to the discussion of the preceding paragraph, as follows:

I	III
it is possible that he is	it is not possible that he is
it is not necessary that he is	it is necessary that he is not
it is not impossible that he is	it is impossible that he is

II	IV
it is possible that he is not	it is not possible that he is not
it is not necessary that he is not	it is necessary that he is
it is not impossible that he is not	it is impossible that he is not

"it is not possible"—I mean, that one contradictory proposition is implied by the other; i.e., the affirmative is implied by the negative. However, they do so inversely—I mean, the negative of the impossible is implied by the affirmative of the possible, and the affirmative of the impossible is implied by the negative of the possible.

72. With the necessary propositions, it is not the 22^a38-22^b1 contradictory but the contrary proposition which is implied by the possible—I mean, the contrary of the affirmative necessary proposition, which contradicts the negative necessary proposition, and this contrary is our sentence "it is necessary that he is not." That is because the negation of this premise—namely, our sentence "it is necessary that he is not," which is implied by our sentence "it is not possible that he is"—is not our sentence "it is not necessary that he is"—which is implied by our sentence "it is possible that he is," as has been set down.[10] That is because it is possible for both of these sentences to be true of one and the same thing. For of what necessarily is not, it is true that it is not necessary that it be.[11] But our sentence "it is necessary that he is not" is the contrary of our sentence "it is necessary that he is"—which is itself the contradiction of our sentence "it is not necessary that he is." If this is so, then one contradictory proposition does not imply another here. Instead one contradictory proposition is implied by the contrary of another contradictory proposition. I mean, it is not the affirmative of the necessary proposition—namely, the contradiction of the negative of the necessary proposition that we posited as being implied by the affirmative of the possible—which is implied by the negative of the possible proposition. Indeed, it is the contrary of the necessary proposition—namely, our sentence "it is necessary that

[10] See above, paras. 69-70.
[11] This could also be translated as: "For of 'it is necessary that he is not,' it is true that 'it is not necessary that he is.' "

he is not"—which is implied by the negative of the possible proposition.

22ᵇ2-11   73. The reason for the negative simple impossible proposition to imply the affirmative of the retractive necessary proposition and for the negative of the retractive possible to imply the affirmative of the simple necessary proposition is that the impossible is the contrary of the existent necessary, even if they both have the same potential with respect to necessity. Now since the negative simple possible proposition implies the affirmative simple impossible proposition and the affirmative simple impossible proposition is the contrary of the affirmative simple necessary proposition, the necessary consequence is that a contrary of the affirmative simple necessary proposition—namely, the affirmative retractive necessary proposition—follows upon it. Moreover, since the negative retractive possible proposition implies the affirmative retractive impossible proposition and the affirmative retractive impossible proposition is a contrary of the affirmative retractive necessary proposition, it follows that with respect to the necessary it implies a contrary of the affirmative retractive necessary proposition—namely, the affirmative simple necessary proposition.

22ᵇ12-21   74. However, if this is followed out, it might be supposed that the case with the way the necessary is implied by the possible is the same as with the way the impossible is implied by it. I mean, that one contradictory implies another, but not according to the first manner the problematic sense of which was explained.[12] So what our sentence "it is possible that he is" implies is our sentence "it is not necessary that he is not"—which is the contradictory of our sentence "it is necessary that he is not," itself implied by our sentence "it is not possible that he is"—not our sentence "it is not necessary that he is." And what our sentence "it is possible that he is not" implies, with respect to

[12] See above, para. 71.

the necessary, is our sentence "it is not necessary that he is," not our sentence "it is not necessary that he is not" as we stipulated when this was first set down.[13]

75. Now how it becomes evident that our sentence "it is possible that he is" implies our sentence "it is not necessary that he is not," not our sentence "it is not necessary that he is," derives from the explanation that our sentence "it is possible that he is" is itself implied by our sentence "it is necessary that he is." And this will become clear from what I say: namely, of our sentence "it is necessary that he is," either our sentence "it is possible that he is" or our sentence "it is not possible that he is" is true. For our sentence "it is possible that he is" and "it is not possible that he is" are two contradictory propositions, and two contradictory propositions divide into truth and falsehood in all things. So if our sentence "it is possible that he is" is not true of it, our sentence "it is not possible that he is" will be true of it. However, if our sentence "it is not possible that he is" is true of it, our sentence "it is impossible that he is" is true of it, since this is implied by our sentence "it is not possible that he is." And if our sentence "it is impossible that he is" is true of it, the implication is that it is impossible for that which is necessary to be. And that is an impossible disparity. Therefore, what is true of our sentence "it is necessary that he is" is our sentence "it is possible that he is." For if one of two contradictory propositions is false, the other is true. 22^b21-28

76. If it has been settled that our sentence "it is possible that he is" is implied by our sentence "it is necessary that he is," then I say: what is implied by our sentence "it is possible that he is" with respect to prem- 22^b29-35

[13] See above, para. 69. In each of these instances—i.e., what is implied by the affirmative simple possible proposition "it is possible that he is" and by the affirmative retractive possible proposition "it is possible that he is not"—the possible proposition is now said to imply a different kind of necessary proposition than was stated in para. 69.

ises of necessity is the negative retractive one—namely, our sentence "it is not necessary that he is not." A demonstrative proof of this is that what is implied by it—I mean, by the affirmative simple possible proposition—can be nothing other than either the negative of the simple necessary proposition, the affirmative of the simple necessary proposition, the affirmative of the retractive necessary proposition, or the negative of the retractive necessary proposition. And if the negative of the simple necessary proposition is as we have posited—namely, our sentence "it is not necessary that he is"[14]—and the affirmative simple possible proposition has been implied by the simple necessary proposition, the consequence is that its contradiction—namely, the negative simple proposition—is implied by the simple necessary proposition. For it brings the sentence forth in this way: it is possible for what exists necessarily to be and it is not necessary for what exists possibly to be.[15] Therefore it is not necessary for what is necessary to exist, which is an impossible disparity. For it is not possible for both contradictory statements to be true.

77. If the negative simple necessary proposition is not implied by it, all that is left is that either the affirmative of the simple necessary proposition or of the retractive proposition[16] or the negative of the retractive necessary proposition be implied by it. However, neither the affirmative of the simple necessary proposition nor of the retractive proposition[16] is true of the affirmative possible proposition.[17] That is because whatever possibly is, either can be or not be. And whatever can be or not be neither necessarily is nor necessarily is not. And that is self-evident. Now if it is

[14] See above, para. 69.
[15] Or, more literally, "for that which is necessarily, it is possible that it is and for that which is possibly, it is not necessary that it is," the idea being that what is necessary is possible and what is possible is not necessary.
[16] That is, the affirmative of the retractive necessary proposition.
[17] That is, the affirmative simple possible proposition.

necessary that the simple possible proposition[17] imply one of the four necessary propositions and it has been explained that it does not imply three of them, then nothing is left for it to imply but our sentence "it is not necessary that he is not"—namely, the negative of the retractive necessary proposition. Moreover, that is necessary because it does not give rise to the absurdity that occurred earlier when we posited that what is not possible is implied by the necessary.[18] And our sentence "it is necessary that he is" may be implied by our sentence "it is not necessary that he is not," since both are true of one thing.

78. However, doubt may occur concerning our explanation that our sentence "it is possible that he is" is implied by our sentence "it is necessary that he is."[19] That is because if it is not implied by it, then its contradiction is. Its contradiction is either our sentence "it is not possible that he is" or our sentence "it is possible that he is not." However, if our sentence "it is not possible that he is" is implied by it, the absurdity we just mentioned is inevitable. And if our sentence "it is possible that he is not" is implied by it, the inevitable result is that what necessarily is may possibly not be, and that is an impossible disparity. So it follows from this argument[20] that what is implied by our sentence "it is necessary that he is" is our sentence "it is possible that he is." However, if we postulate that our sentence "it is possible that he is" is what is implied by it and if anything which possibly is possibly is not, it is inevitable that whatever necessarily is can possibly be and not be. And that is an impossible disparity. Now if the first argument[20] affirms that what is implied by our sentence "it is necessary that he is" is our sentence "it is possible that he is" and the second denies that the possible follows the necessary and is implied by it, then

---

[18] See above, para. 75.
[19] See above, para. 75.
[20] This is the same word (qawl) which has been translated elsewhere as "sentence" and "saying."

it is clear that what the first argument[20] established about it being of the nature of the possible to be implied by the necessary must be other than what the second rejects.

22ᵇ36-23ᵃ6   79. Therefore, "possible" is said of more than one idea, and that also becomes clear through induction. It is evident that not everything of which it is said "it is possible that it does or receives[21] like this" has the power not to do and to do. That is because the things that we say have powers to do are of two types: either powers linked with reason, and they are expressed as capability; or powers not linked with reason, like fire heating and ice cooling. The powers linked with reason include that of doing contrary things, I mean, of doing and not doing. An example of that is walking, for man equally has the power to walk and not walk. The powers not linked with reason only include that of doing one of the contrary things. Fire is an example of that, for it only has the power of heating, not that of not heating—except accidentally. The latter occurs either whenever it finds no subject to receive the heat or whenever an impediment prevents it from doing what it naturally does to that subject. Some distinct non-rational powers may be found which equally receive the two opposites. If this is so, then not every possible can receive opposite things.

23ᵃ7-17   80. Nor is the possible one of the things spoken of synonymously as though it were a single species, but the term "possible" is one of the things spoken of ambiguously.[22] That is because we may say "possible" of what is actually existent, and our saying of it that it is

---

[21] "Receives" in the sense of receiving an action or being acted upon; see above, *Middle Commentary on Aristotle's Categories*, para. 84.

[22] Or, perhaps, "homonymously" *bi-ishtirāk al-ism*. Aristotle uses the term "homonyms" (*omōnumoi*) in the corresponding passage, a term Averroes usually translates as *asmā muttafiqah*. However, when commenting on Aristotle's definition of homonyms, Averroes suggests that *asmā muttafiqah* and *asmā mushtarikah* can be used interchangeably; see above, para. 57, note 33 and paras. 58-59; see also *Middle Commentary on Aristotle's Categories*, para. 3.

possible only means that this condition actually existing
for it was possible for it or else it would not have received it. And this may be said even if the possibility
of it does not temporally precede actuality, if something of this description exists. Possible is said of other
things with the meaning that they are such as to exist
in the future. Now this possibility is found only in
moving things, whether they pass away or not. However, with respect to things that do not pass away, its
occurrence is necessary—like the sun rising tomorrow.
And with respect to things that do pass away, its coming
into being is not necessary.

81. The second sort of possible is found in non-
moving things. This sort of possible is the one which
is implied by the necessary. The first sort, which concerns things that pass away, is not implied by the necessary. However, this may seem to be the same as saying that since the possible is more general than the
necessary—because it applies to the necessary and the
non-necessary—it follows that it is implied by it the
way the more general is implied by the more particular,
I mean, the way animal is implied by man.[23]

82. He said: since the varieties of the possible have
been explained, we must set down our saying "it is
necessary that he is," "it is not necessary that he is" as
the first thing used for rational comparison in these
implications. For it is the principle of all these things.[24]
Then we will consider what the remaining propositions
imply.

23ᵃ18-21

83. He said: this is something that was done in the
Prior Analytics, so we shall postpone the matter until
that discussion.[25] The necessary is surely the principle

23ᵃ22-27

---

[23] See above, paras. 43 and 47.

[24] That is, the necessary and the not necessary are the primary
concepts from which the other modalities—possibility and impos-
sibility—are derived.

[25] Literally, "that place" (dhālika al-mawḍiʿ). See Aristotle Prior
Analytics I.ii-iii.25ᵃ1-25ᵇ26 and Averroes Middle Commentary on Aristotle's Prior Analytics, paras. 20-23.

of these things, because necessary things are eternally existent in actuality—as is explained in the theoretical sciences. And since eternal things are prior, it follows that things which are actual are prior to things which are actual at one time and potential at another time. Therefore some beings exist in actuality, not in potentiality—like the first being. And some are actual at one time and potential at another time, namely, things which come into being and pass away. And some things are only potential and are never free of it, like motion and in general the unending insofar as it is unending, as was explained in natural science.[26]

84. This is the sum of what he said about propositions having modal inflections.

[26] Or "physics" (*al-'ilm al-ṭabī'ī*). For Aristotle's discussions of these questions, see *Metaphysics* IX.vi.1048ᵃ32-1048ᵇ37 and IX.viii.1049ᵇ4-1051ᵃ3; also *Physics* III.vi.206ᵃ9-207ᵃ32.

CHAPTER FIVE

85. He said: opposite[1] sentences are opposite either   23ᵃ28-31
through affirmation and negation or through their
material elements being contraries—namely, sentences
whose predicates are contrary. Among those whose
predicates are contraries are found some which resemble the five sorts of opposition with respect to affirmation and negation which were discussed earlier.[2]
Because of all this, we must inquire here as to which
sentences are more contrary and more dissimilar with
respect to belief: is it those which are contraries by way
of affirmation and negation or those which are contraries by way of belief in the contrary? For example,
two sentences are opposed to our sentence "every man
is just." One of them is "not a single man is just,"
namely, the opposite with respect to negation. And the
second is our sentence "every man is unjust," namely,
the opposite with respect to what is contrary. So which
one of these two is more contrary to our sentence "every
man is just": is it our sentence "not a single man is
just" or our sentence "every man is unjust"?

86. We say: if utterances signify only ideas arising   23ᵃ33-23ᵇ2
in the soul and there already exists in the mind belief
in a certain thing and belief in its contrary or belief in
a certain thing and belief in its negation, then it is clear
that a sentence is said to be the contrary of a sentence
or its opposite with respect to the beliefs in the soul
being opposed only because of belief in the contrary
or because of belief in the negation. If the matter is
like that, then we ought to inquire as to which belief
is most extremely contrary and dissimilar to the true

---

[1] This is the beginning of a long conditional sentence whose apodosis is the clause "because of all this . . . belief in the contrary."

[2] See above, para. 23.

or false belief: is it the belief in its contrary or the belief in its negation? For example, if we believe that a certain thing is good and that belief is true—like our belief that life is good—then there are two false beliefs here which are opposed to it. One is that it is evil, and the other is that it is not good. Now which of these two false beliefs about life is the one which is in our mind most extremely contrary to the true belief, namely, our saying "life is good": is it our belief that it is evil or our belief that it is not good?

87. We say: the contrary existing in the belief—I mean, the one most extremely dissimilar to it—resembles the contrary existing outside the soul in material things. So does it necessarily follow that those things which are most contrary outside the soul are most contrary in belief?

23ᵇ3-7   88. We say: since two things which, contrary in two ways outside the soul, are less contrary in belief than two things which are contrary in one way and are, moreover, not contrary in belief but even mutually imply each other—like our belief that life is good and death is evil, for these two sentences are contrary in terms of predicate and subject outside the soul—it is clear that the cause of the contrary existing in belief is not the contrary existing outside the soul. For if it were the cause, what is more contrary outside the soul would be more likely to be contrary in belief. If that is so, then the contrary in belief arising from material things is more likely not to be what is simply contrary in belief. And the contrary existing in belief because of affirmation and negation does not come about because of anything else, but because of itself and because of a condition existing in it in the mind. So what is contrary because of itself is more likely to be contrary than what is contrary because of something else.

23ᵇ8-14   89. Moreover, if we have a certain belief about something to the effect that it is good and it is a true belief, then not every false belief we may have about that thing is a belief contrary to this true belief—like our ascribing something else to it which really does not pertain to it or not ascribing something else which does pertain to it—for beliefs are endless. But there is only one belief which is contrary to that belief, namely, the belief which we think always divides into truth and falsehood along with the first belief. And these are the two beliefs which are stipulated to be the two parts of the contradiction in a problem and concerning which there later arises uncertainty and perplexity as to which one is true and which false. Now there can be no uncertainty and perplexity about two beliefs which can both be false or both true with respect to one and the same subject. Nor can they be made the two parts of the contradiction with respect to a problem in such a way that what is true about one of them definitely exists in itself even if it is not definite for us. Moreover, it is clear that the belief which is truly opposed to being is the belief in the thing from which generation[3] comes about—namely, negation. That is because generation is from non-being to being, and passing away is from being to non-being.

90. Belief about things in which alteration occurs—   23^{b}15-27 that is, change occurring in contraries—is of less contrariety. For non-existence is more an opposite of existence than one contrary is of another, because the contrary is a kind of existent thing. Therefore coming into being is only accidentally part of being. Moreover, belief that comes into being by means of the negation requires the affirmative belief itself to be eliminated, for the quiddity[4] of the negation requires the elimination of the affirmation, which is an imitation of the existent thing. Yet the quiddity of belief in the contrary of the predicate with respect to something whose predicate is believed to exist does not require that the affirmation be eliminated, for the occurrence of the con-

---

[3] This is the word which has been translated elsewhere as "coming to be" (kawn).

[4] See above, *Middle Commentary on Aristotle's Categories*, para. 8, note 3.

trary in the subject does not in and of itself[5] require that the contrary opposed to it be eliminated. Indeed, this is something which happens due to its occurring in the subject—I mean, that one contrary be eliminated by the advent of another. For example, the elimination of heat from water by the advent of cold is ascribed to cold as a secondary intention or as an accident. That is because this instance of elimination arises[6] from existence, and the elimination with respect to the negation is elimination arising[7] from the negation itself. What implies the elimination of the affirmation itself is more likely to be the contrariety existing in belief than what implies it accidentally or as a secondary intention, and it is more perfectly and more strongly contrary. If the two contraries are two extremely differing things and the contrary which is in the mind of the affirmed thing due to contradiction is stronger than the contrary of it due to belief in its contrary existing outside the soul, then it is clear that belief in the contradiction is the belief simply contrary to the affirmation. Moreover, the belief that something good is evil implies another belief—namely, that it is not good. And the belief that something good is not good does not imply another belief—I mean, that it is evil. If that is so, there is no contrary belief with respect to things that have no contrary.

23ᵇ28-32   91. Therefore, belief in the negation is more generally contrary to the affirmation than belief in the contrary. And it is contrariety in itself, since it exists for things which have a contrary and for those which do not have a contrary. Thus, it follows that the belief which is by nature contrary to the affirmation is the belief which exists as a contrary in every situation, not in one situation and not another. The general belief which is contrary in every situation and in itself is more strongly contrary than the belief which is contrary in

---

[5] Literally, "by its substance" (*bi-jawharih*).

[6] Or "occurs" (*ḥādith*).

[7] Or "occurring" (*ḥādith*).

one situation and not another, for the general is naturally prior to the particular. Therefore if the particular exists, the general exists; but not the converse, I mean, that if the general exists, the particular exists. Thus if it is the negation which is contrary in belief to what has no contrary, it follows that it is the negation which is contrary in every situation—that is, in the extreme.

92. Moreover, the belief that something good is good   23ᵇ33-24ᵃ3
and the belief that something not good is not good are two true beliefs. And the belief that something not good is good or that something good is not good are two false beliefs. Now which belief—would that I knew— is contrary to our belief that something not good is not good, which is a true belief? It admits of only three cases. One is that what is contrary to it is the belief in its contrary—namely, the belief that something not good is evil. The second is that what is contrary is the negation of the contrary—namely, the belief that something not good is not evil. The third is that what is contrary to the belief that something is not good is that it is good. Now belief in its contrary is not a contrary to it in belief. That is because both can be true. For many things which are not good are evil. And belief in the negation of its contrary is not a belief contrary to it either, for both may be true of a single thing. Thus that it is neither good nor evil is true of the line and in general of whatever is not such as to have one of these two contraries attributed to it. If that is so, then the belief contrary to our belief that something not good is not good is our belief that something not good is good. And if the belief which is most extremely contrary to our belief that something not good is not good is our belief that it is good, then the contrary most extremely dissimilar to our belief that something good is good is our belief that it is not good—not our belief that it is evil. For if the affirmation is what is most extremely contrary to the negation, then it must be most extremely remote from it. If that is so and a

contrary has only a single contrary, then what is most
extremely contrary to affirmation is negation.

24ᵃ4-9   93. He said: with propositions like those we used
here, which are contrary as negations and affirmations,
there is no difference between uttering them with the
subject denoted by the *alif* and the *lām*[8] or uttering
them with it limited by the universal limitation. For we
have already said that the *alif* and the *lām*[8] may signify
what the universal limitation signifies.[9] So in this sense
there is no difference between our saying "the contrary
of the belief about what is good is that it is not good"
and our saying "the contrary of the belief about everything which is good is that not a single thing is good."
That is because affirmation and negation—that is, the
contrary belief—only exist in the soul for the universal
meaning.

24ᵇ1-6   94. If what comes out as an utterance signifies which
of the two contrary beliefs is in the soul, then it is clear
that the contrary of the articulated[10] affirmation is the
articulated[10] negation of that same universal meaning
which the affirmation signifies when it signifies the
universal meaning affirmatively or negatively by means
of the universal utterance—namely, the limitation. For
example, the contrary of our saying "every man is good"
is our saying "not a single man is good," and its contradiction is "not every man is good."

24ᵇ7-9   95. It is clear[11] that the beliefs said to be contrary
here cannot be true beliefs, for it is not possible that
one truth be contrary to another, nor that one true
belief be contrary to another, nor that one utterance
be contradictory of another when both signify an idea
which is in itself true. Rather, contrary beliefs are those
in opposition through affirmation and negation, as well
as those which are contradictory and contrary in the

---

[8] Or "the"; see above, para. 24, notes 4 and 5.

[9] The reference is to para. 24 above.

[10] Literally, "the uttered" (*fī al-lafẓ*).

[11] Or, depending on the vowelization, "he explained" (*huwa bayyin*
or *huwa bayyan*).

necessary mood. That is because with many opposites it is possible—as has been said[12]—that both be true—namely, the indeterminate and those subordinate to the contrary. Now it is not possible for both contraries to be true about one and the same thing, nor is it possible for both to be false in the necessary mood, since the subject is not removed from them.[13]

96. With the completion of the ideas contained in this book, the middle commentary on the ideas contained in this book here ends.

[12] See para. 24.
[13] That is, since both have the same subject.

INDEX

accident, 13-17, 25, 26, 28, 29,
  32-38, 65, 129, 184
Ackrill, J. L., xviii, 14
actual, 180
affection, 61, 63-65; affective
  quality, 61, 63-65
affirmation, 26, 30, 79, 101, 102,
  125, 131, 136, 137, 139-144,
  147, 154, 159, 161, 162, 169,
  181-186; affirmative, 72, 73, 76,
  80, 108, 109, 111, 113, 137,
  140, 150, 154, 161, 173
al-Ahwānīy, Fuʾād, 5
al-Fārābī, xi, 3, 5, 16, 36, 70, 128,
  134, 135; *Kitāb al-Alfāẓ al-
  Mustaʿmalah fī al-Manṭiq*, 128;
  Kitāb al-Ḥurūf, 135
al-Kindī, xi
Albertus Magnus, xi
Alcuin, x
Alexander of Aphrodisias, xi
Alexandria, x, xi
Amīn, ʿUthmān, 5
Andronikus of Rhodes, x, xii
Antioch, xi
Apellikon, ix
Archbishop St. Ouen of Rouen, x
Aristotle, ix-xiii, xv, xvii-xix, 4-18,
  25, 35, 46, 56, 58, 70, 72, 73,
  76, 78, 85, 91-102, 106-117,
  125, 128, 132, 136, 137, 154,
  178-181, 186; *Categories*, x, xiii,
  xviii, 6, 7, 10, 11, 25, 91, 104,
  116; *De Anima*, 94, 95, 125; *De
  Interpretatione*, x, xiii, xiv, 6, 91,
  93-99, 103, 106-110, 113, 114,
  132; *Metaphysics*, 5, 16, 35, 58,

180; *On Sophistical Refutations*,
  ix, 136; *Organon*, xiv; *Physics*,
  46, 180; *Poetics*, ix, 131-133;
  Posterior Analytics, ix, xiii, xiv,
  133; *Prior Analytics*, ix, x, xiii,
  xiv, 110, 116, 134, 154, 158;
  Rhetoric, ix, 132, 133; *Topics*, ix,
  14, 35, 105, 163; he mentioned,
  128; he said, 26, 27, 29, 30, 34,
  45, 49, 50, 52, 56, 58-60, 62,
  63, 65-71, 73, 75, 79-82, 85, 86,
  125, 131, 179-181, 186
Athens, x
Averroes (Ibn Rushd), ix, xi-xx,
  3, 4, 6-18, 25, 45, 58, 60, 67,
  75, 83, 91-117, 131, 137, 151,
  154, 156, 158, 164, 172, 178,
  179, 181, 182; *Kitāb al-Samāʿ
  al-Ṭabīʿīy*, 5; *Long Commentary
  on Aristotle's Metaphysics*, 35;
  *Long Commentary on Aritstotle's
  Physics*, 4, 5; *Long Commentary on
  Aristotle's Posterior Analytics*, 4;
  *Middle Commentary on Aristotle's
  Categories*, xii-xiv, xvii, xix, 5, 7-
  12, 14-17, 87, 104, 129, 137,
  151, 153, 155, 161, 162, 166,
  178, 183; *Middle Commentary on
  Aristotle's De Interpretatione*, xvii,
  xix, 91; *Middle Commentary on
  Aristotle's Prior Analytics*, 134,
  154, 158, 179; *Middle Commentary on Aristotle's Rhetoric*, xiv,
  105; *Middle Commentary on Aristotle's Topics*, 105, 106, 163;
  Rasāʾil, 5; *Short Commentary on
  Aristotle's Logic*, 12, 14; *Short*